I hope you will find something in this book that will give you a laugh, a tear, some encouragement, or a spiritual blessing.

MATTHEW 6:33

God bless

Dick

James Richard (Dick) Anthony

To
From

WINNING PERSPECTIVES
IN PICTURE & RHYME

Poems featuring hope and joy now and for all time

James Richard Anthony

Winning Perspectives in Picture & Rhyme
Poems featuring hope and joy now and for all time

ISBN: 978-0-578-58472-0

Published by Providential, LLC

winningperspectivesinrhyme@gmail.com

Printed in the United States of America

Editors

Janet Bangs

Ashley Heinemeyer

Page Designer

Lissa Auciello-Brogan

Permissions and Citations

Ashley Heinemeyer

Project Manager

Judy Miller

Contributors

Suzanne Mueller

Julie Cooley

Cover design and photo editing

Clint Lahnen

Table of Contents

About the Author

James Richard Anthony is founder of IMMI, an industry leader in the design, testing and manufacturing of advanced safety systems. He started in business with his father in 1956, with Uniform Hood Lace, a company that produces anti-squeak material for classic automobiles. He also established IMMI's Word and Deed Foundation. He and his wife, Beverly, live near Westfield, Indiana and have four children and eight grandchildren.

For more information or to obtain copies of this book and others written by James Richard Anthony please email, winningperspectivesinrhyme@gmail.com.

Acknowledgments

First and foremost, this book would not be possible without the Lord's many blessings. He has surrounded me with amazingly creative and encouraging people. I'm grateful for their incredible talents and faithful hearts. Together our love for Him brings life to this book.

This team begins with my wonderful wife **Bev Anthony**. She is my devoted partner and most understanding friend through life. Bev has served as my "Editor-in-Chief" through this great journey in writing. She is indeed the wind beneath my wings.

I want to also thank and acknowledge the following team who've provided so much support:

Janet Bangs served as a primary editor, helping to refine these poems before our layout even began.

Lissa Auciello-Brogan gave us wise counsel and developed the overall book design and layout.

Julie Cooley's professional expertise has been invaluable in adding the final finesse and polish.

Ashley Heinemeyer offered the picture and illustration perspective needed for publishing and planning, as well as remarkable spiritual input and expertise in publishing details.

Clint Lahnen designed our cover, as well as providing his talents with photo editing.

Judy Miller poured out her continued encouragement, while directing and coordinating our communications.

Suzanne Mueller used her God-given gifts and faithful counsel to help make this book better than we envisioned.

WHEN ALL NATURE SINGS

When wind whispers through needles of a white pine tree,
I hear His spirit speak peace in a gentle minor key.

I sense His voice in the gurgle of a rocky babbling brook,
Birds sing melodies as if from His heavenly song book.

As I meditate on His goodness in the beauty of nature's sound,
My soul rejoices and escapes the unrest the world's system is
putting down.

I feel free from the cares and burdens I bring Him,
For the spirit breathes assurance of His love and cleansing
from my sin.

Now even the noisy crow and the blue jay's discordant call,
Fade into a joyful hymn praising God for the wonder of it all.

...but the Holy Spirit prays for us with such feeling that it cannot be expressed in words.

Romans 8:26b TLB

If we confess our sins, he is faithful and just and will forgive us our sins and purify us from all unrighteousness.

1 John 1:9 NIV

Wash away all my iniquity and cleanse me from my sin.

Psalm 51:2 NIV

Do not love the world or the things in the world.

1 John 2:15a NKJV

The Mansions' Message

I strolled by a magnificent old mansion today,
And wondered what it would be like to live that way.

The home was a museum on a beautiful hill,
So I decided to go in and pick up a thrill.

When I reached the grand entrance and
opened the door,
I did not realize this adventure could
turn to much more.

The decor inside was something to behold,
With gold and glitter rich merchants
had sold.

I joined a small group for the guided tour,
And was assured false opulence would
soon find a cure.

Through a hundred rooms I strolled
till quite bored,
As I took in fine sights which the
owners adored.

When we came to the kitchen and
dining room there,
I could hardly grasp the sight of
such fine fare.

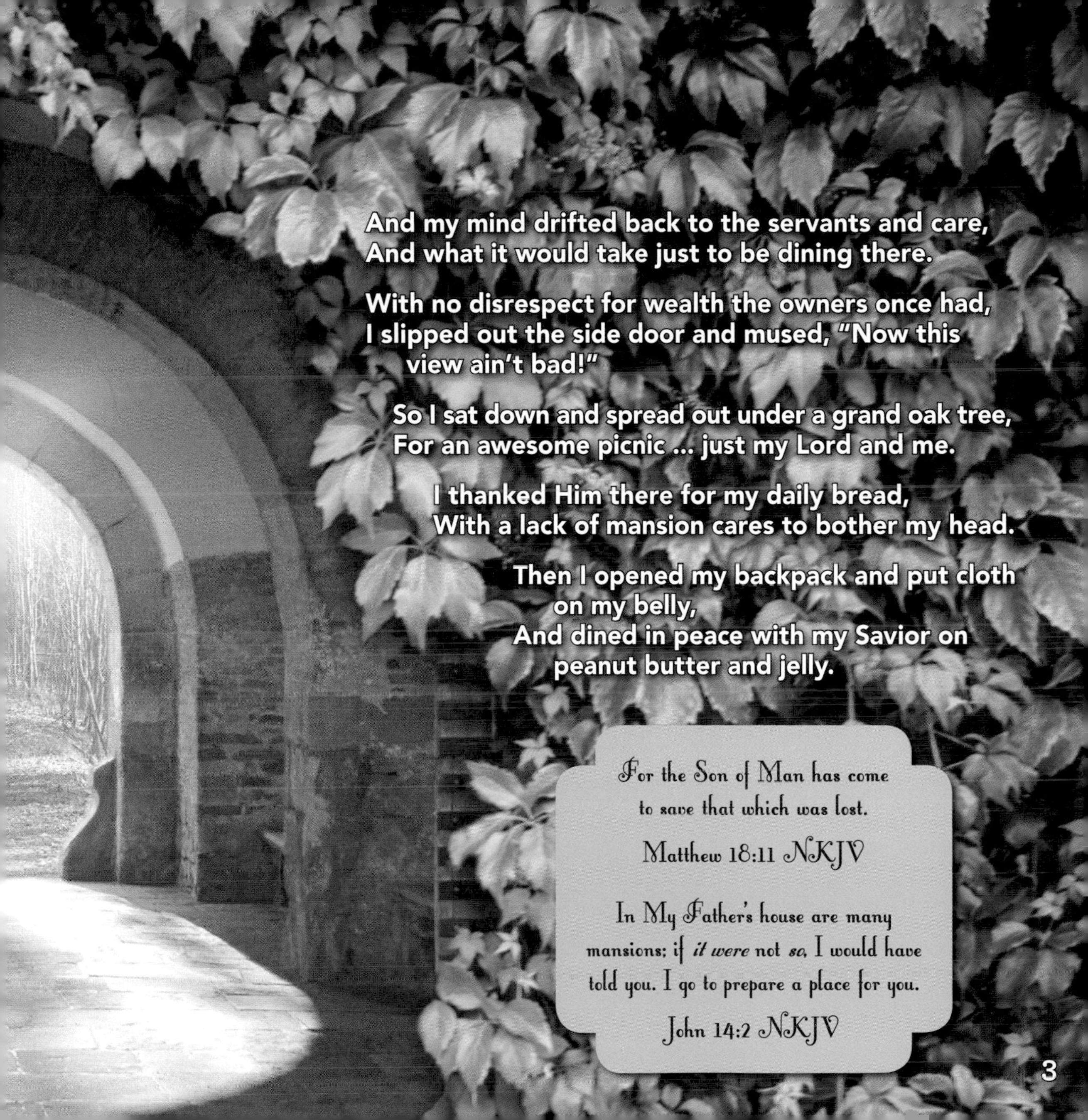

And my mind drifted back to the servants and care,
And what it would take just to be dining there.

With no disrespect for wealth the owners once had,
I slipped out the side door and mused, "Now this view ain't bad!"

So I sat down and spread out under a grand oak tree,
For an awesome picnic … just my Lord and me.

I thanked Him there for my daily bread,
With a lack of mansion cares to bother my head.

Then I opened my backpack and put cloth on my belly,
And dined in peace with my Savior on peanut butter and jelly.

For the Son of Man has come
to save that which was lost.

Matthew 18:11 NKJV

In My Father's house are many
mansions; if *it were* not *so,* I would have
told you. I go to prepare a place for you.

John 14:2 NKJV

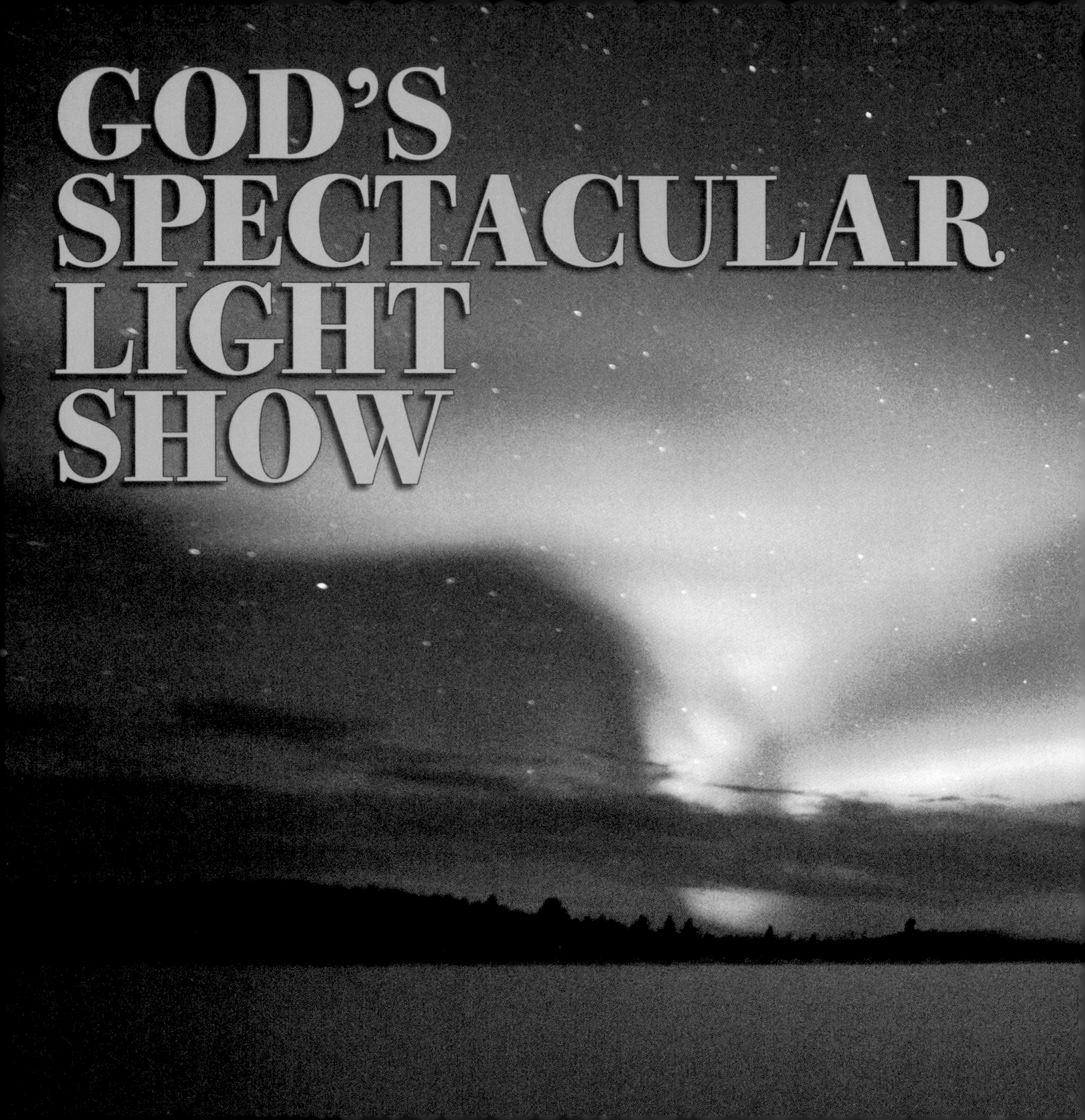
GOD'S
SPECTACULAR
LIGHT
SHOW

When the green and red curtains fall over the northern sky,
You feel a stirring in your soul as you seek to understand why.

For as these beautiful flowing draperies cast a breathtaking sight,
Your heart gains a small glimpse of God's Omnipotence and Might.

For when Northern Lights shimmer and glow on a dark moonless night,
You can't help but thank God for eyes to behold this awesome delight.

As you watch in rapt attention while they perform without a sound,
You may find you have been captured as they circle all around.

And while the pretty light castles hold you captive and descend on every side,
They now reflect below in the still lake leaving your gaze no place to hide.

The stars shine through this splendor as pretty diamonds now turned soft and pale,
Each one highlighting God's great love like a bride's smile behind her veil.

And could it be that gentle stirring is the Holy Spirit's touch upon your heart,
With a sure hope to reflect God's glory someday where you will never part?

The heavens declare the glory of God,
and the firmament shows His handiwork.

Psalm 19:1 NKJV

These things I have written to you who
believe in the name of the Son of God, that
you may know that you have eternal life.

1 John 5:13a NKJV

Delayed Beauty

Hidden inside summer's leaves all dressed in green,
Are bright fall colors which are not yet to be seen.

Till the tinge of fall brings change to our view,
And restful green leaves are colored many a hue.

Scientists tell us the colors were there all the while,
But cannot be seen till God's Autumn turns the dial.

And many a young life seems to run a parallel course,
With no promise foreseen and sad feelings of remorse.

Till a touch of the Master's hand is their guide,
And we see that great talent in them does abide.

For their soul now is bright with love, joy, and peace,
And it is apparent their life has an everlasting new lease.

While winter's chill ultimately brings the brown leaves to the earth,
The Christian's Soul lives on and has been given new birth.

And while all lives are shaded with happy and difficult seasons,
We can know God's grace permits both for His love-reasons.

So, Christian, pursue what the Holy Spirit puts down inside,
And His awesome love gifts will be seen in you here and eternally abide.

But the Holy Spirit produces this kind of fruit in our lives: love, joy, peace, patience, kindness, goodness, faithfulness, gentleness, and self-control. There is no law against these things!

Galatians 5:22-23 NLT

Wild Walleye Pike

Walleye Pike, delicious! beautiful?
The first time I saw a walleye, I was but a young lad,
And I thought that prehistoric fish sure did look bad.

And I marveled at the weapons walleyes have at their command,
For their dorsal fins, gill plates, and sharp teeth can sure cut up one's hand.

When fishing I found their bite so soft they coax the bait right off your line,
But at other times they bite so wildly they get hooked every time.

But if you are ever treated to a North Woods' shore lunch,
You will find walleye the best eating fish of the bunch.

So I apologize to God for any disrespect to the walleye's look,
As I remember Jesus made all the fish, not just the ones His disciples took.

It is funny how my perspective has changed to an entirely different view,
For now when I see walleye under my boat, they are a beautiful thing to pursue.

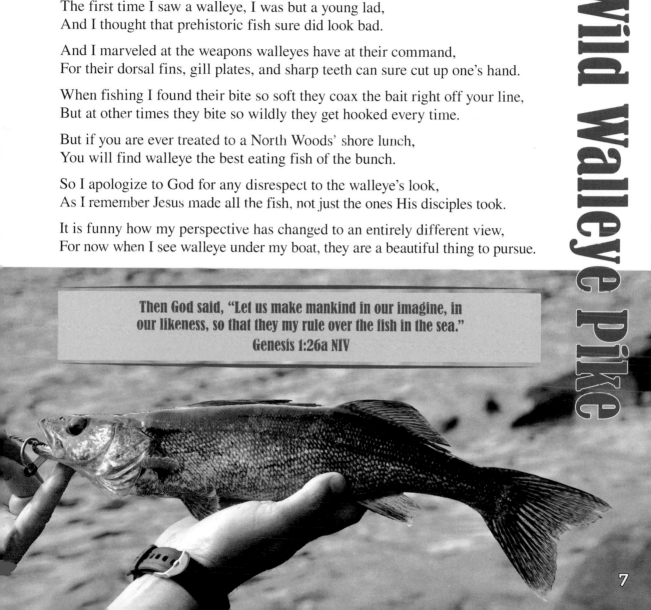

Then God said, "Let us make mankind in our imagine, in our likeness, so that they my rule over the fish in the sea."
Genesis 1:26a NIV

Kayak Fellowship

I kayaked early on the calm lake today,
Enjoying the heavy cloud of fog on my way.

As the bow of my boat parted water so calm,
My soul took rest in this amazing soul balm.

And where sounds of motors often abound,
I heard nothing but gentle lapping of water all around.

And the soothing cry of a loon to her chicks,
Was surely a contrast from angry gulls in the mix.

When the water swirled as I disturbed a big fish,
I had no pole by my side to consider making him a dish.

Only gentle sounds whispered to my soul "Just be at rest.
Use this precious time in the way you know best."

And as the fog now gently washed over my face,
I was so grateful to be part of His forgiven human race.

Then it seemed as if someone had joined me on board,
And my mind's eye perceived, it must be the Lord.

For as the shore not seen, but I knew to be there,
My Savior's sure presence the Spirit made aware.

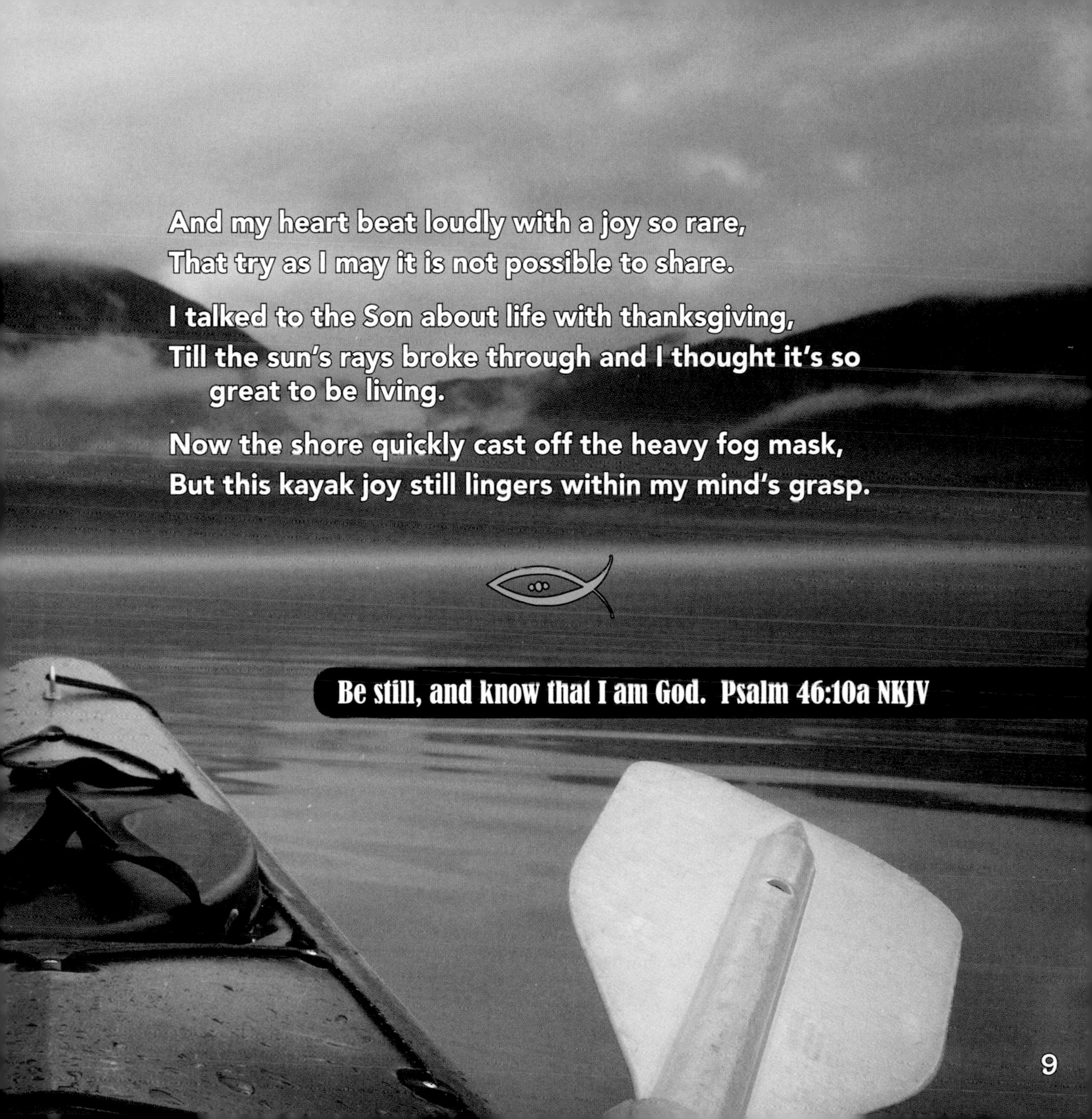

And my heart beat loudly with a joy so rare,
That try as I may it is not possible to share.

I talked to the Son about life with thanksgiving,
Till the sun's rays broke through and I thought it's so
great to be living.

Now the shore quickly cast off the heavy fog mask,
But this kayak joy still lingers within my mind's grasp.

Be still, and know that I am God. Psalm 46:10a NKJV

Refreshing
Perspective

Be it beautiful blue sky or rippling stream,
They are all part of the Master's magnificent scene.

And it is great to slip away from the crowded city view,
To meditate on God's awesome creation and perspective anew.

The hustle and bustle of the city's pull toward earthly reward,
Can leave one exhausted or even feeling quite bored.

When reminded again of God's creative authority,
It can align one's goals and give projects proper priority.

We see God's nature does prosper with little care from our hand,
While the birds sing His praises and flowers decorate His land.

And though His Genesis command grants man dominion over it all,
When we stray from the Holy Spirit's control, our joy and peace is sure to fall.

So Jesus reminds us to take note of God's great care,
As we view the flowers in the field and the birds in the air.

To escape day-to-day constant big city strife,
Try a prayer-walk in the park to bring Divine perspective to life.

But remember, if you know Jesus as your Savior and Lord,
Sharing your faith here brings true joy to others with an eternal reward.

You will keep *him* in perfect
peace, *Whose* mind *is* stayed *on*
You, Because he trusts in You.

Isaiah 26:3 NKJV

Lighting a Candle

Be filled with the Spirit.
Ephesians 5:18b NIV

When Jesus spoke again to the people, he said, "I am the light of the world. Whoever follows me will never walk in darkness, but will have the light of life."
John 8:12 NIV

This is the confidence we have in approaching God: that if we ask anything according to His will, He hears us.
1 John 5:14 NIV

How can I possibly be a candle for God today?
For I don't feel a burn in my heart leading that way.

Some worries have slipped in to discourage my walk,
And bid me be weary and careful with my God-talk.

But there are hungry hearts all around, some I have known for so long.
Who today from my lips might hear the sweet Gospel song?

And how when sharing Christ's Love could my soul be cast down?
When I know what freedom and peace in Him can be found.

So I shall pray for the Holy Spirit's blessed control,
And remember the Bible command to give Him the empowerment role.

My Lord came to seek and save all those who are lost,
And bids me tell the love story of our Salvation's great cost.

God has promised to hear my prayer and extend His hand,
If my request is in line with His clear Bible command.

So I shall camp on two Bible verses as I go through this day,
And watch for Spiritual Appointments, He may bring my way.

The candle of faith He has again lit in my heart,
And put a smile on my face and great joy in my heart.

I thank God for perspective which gave my day a new start,
As I'm now prepared for sharing opportunities the Spirit's guidance may impart.

Through the Eyes of a Child

"Let the children come to me;
do not hinder them, for to such
belongs the kingdom of God."

Mark 10:14 ESV

"Look! I stand at the door and
knock. If you hear my voice and
open the door, I will come in."

Revelation 3:20a NLT

Little Betsy's eye was on beauty; she saw it everywhere,
And when she was in a garden, it was every flower beware.

It's not that she was unappreciative or devoted to their harm,
Her eyes just caught their beauty and were fascinated by their charm.

One day she ran home with tulips excited for me to see,
With her smiling eyes she asked, "Who made these flowers for me?"

"They are beautiful, Daddy, and the Maker must love me so much."
I replied, "The flowers in Mr. Smith's garden you must never again touch."

She picked roses in the park, "Daddy, who made these for me? I just have to know?
I love the colors and they smell so good, He must truly love me so!"

I replied, pointing to the gardener who was carefully working the soil,
"You must not pick them, Betsy, for you will upset his toil."

We crossed to a lot where Betsy could pick flowers without care,
And she fashioned a bouquet of violets and put them in her hair.

I said, "You look pretty, dear, and no one cares where these violets go."
Then she said, "Who made them, Daddy? He must truly love us so."

A quick answer I gave to the questioning heart of my child,
"I guess Mother Nature gets credit for the flowers which grow wild."
But by the look on her face I could see her dismay.
She did not appreciate my silly fairy tale answer that day.

So we sat together on the grass and I told her of the Creator,
"He made us and all things and no one's love could be greater."

We talked about the Lord Jesus she was really wanting to know,
And when I told how He saved us, she said, "Oh, He does truly love me so."

But then a lesson followed from my daughter's face so sweet,
For she said, "Daddy, I know His flowers above will be an indescribable treat!"

"For the flowers here have been whispering of the One I now know and adore,
And I'm so happy that Jesus kept knocking and standing at my heart's door."

Hidden in a String

What amazing sounds God has locked up in a string,
And when they are put in a tight span how they can sing.

As a master's bow caresses the violin's strings,
It can coax the love out of your heart which lies deep within.

A string's beautiful sound from a high quivering note,
Can unlock sweeter feelings than almost any pen ever wrote.

If accompanying strings are held under the master's finger,
It can bring tears to your eyes and cause strong emotions to linger.

God sure blessed us when He brought these sweet sounds about,
And granted some the passion and talent to draw music out.

But as we marvel at His great love and the notes hidden in the string,
We can thank Him for ears and hearts to hear the great music they bring.

It takes passion to bring the notes and chords of the music out,
So He gives man keys to His musical storehouse to bring this about.

When He gave us dominion over all the things of His earth,
He blessed some with special talent to give string-music birth.

So if there is a stirring in your soul to make music from strings,
You may find His musical gift to be your perfect thing.

And while He gives us freedom to make strings sing our beautiful song,
Let's not forget to use our talent praising Him as we will in heaven before long.

The heavens declare the glory of God, and the firmament shows His handiwork.

Psalm 19:1 NKJV

Praise Him with stringed instruments and flutes!

Psalm 150:4b NKJV

A Tribute to Shadow

When God made my dog it is easy to see,
He must have been really thinking of me.

For how could I find an animal so true,
Which would lick my face and my feet too.

And join me in slumber, if he can sneak in my bed,
Or who would stay by my side, if I was alive or was dead.

Who almost knocks me over with the wag of his tail,
To let me know he is happy to go with me down
any trail.

His focus on my movement makes sure he misses
no pat,
Even when I am too busy or feeding that old cat.

A good dog's life is built around you,
Shadow's watch is focused on all that I do.

And as his eyes perceive what acts of affection may be,
I think how God must feel when He sees such a heart in me.

When my perspective is in line with Bible reading,
I will rally to actions where the Holy Spirit is leading.

And as I view Shadow's loyalty lesson sent from above,
I seek to be more responsive to God's great redeeming love.

And now abide faith, hope, love, these three; but the greatest of these *is* love.
1 Corinthians 13:13 NKJV

A Sheep's Prayer

As the deer pants for the water brooks, so pants my soul for you, O God.

Psalm 42:1 NKJV

"I am the good shepherd. The good shepherd gives His life for the sheep."

John 10:11 NKJV

Lord, I desire to be one of Your sheep today,
And be led by Your grace along life's way.

Please free me from worry and fear as I go,
And may trust in Your love be all that I know.

If I am tempted to stray down a bad course of sin,
May Your salvation and forgiveness provide a sure win.

And if arrogance in me raises its ugly head,
May Your teaching on humility strike my pride dead.

May I perceive why God paid the highest-ever cost,
So He could seek and save His sheep which are lost.

Help me witness and care for wayward sheep on my way,
As the Holy Spirit shepherds my path and speech this day.

And when nighttime recalls the kind way You have led,
May sleep find this sheep praising my Shepherd in bed.

The History Teacher's Dream

While preparing a history lesson, she gazed out the train window at a parallel track,
But the train's gentle rock bid, "Close your eyes for a moment and just settle back."

Soon she was sound asleep and dreaming of how America's soul was formed,
And then men of differing faiths and philosophies took to a debate floor.

The first argued that all gods should be banned and put aside,
"We must be the captains of an American ship where no deities abide."

"Fine" said another, "but let's proclaim all animals as equal,
For we may be cows or chickens if our lives have a sequel."

But a third said, "Wait! A firm governmental religion must rule over us all,
For my prophet declares, "Death to those who ignore his strict call."

Then a true Founding Father spoke and hushed the diverse band,
"Remember, men, it was Christian faith and courage which lead us to this great land."

"Our Charter must reflect the love, joy, and peace of the Bible,
For "Jesus The Savior" is the only one who can assure America's survival."

But the first speaker said, "Now who can reconcile all these diverse views of religion?
That's why I put faith in myself and hold to my atheistic position."

Then another true Founding Father said, "Christianity is no mere religion or political
control device,
But a personal relationship with the One True God, King, and Sacrifice."

Righteousness exalts a nation, but sin *is* a reproach to *any* people.
Proverbs 14:34 NKJV

The fool has said in his heart, "*There is* no God."
Psalm 14:1 NKJV

"And belief in a religion of self as a none won't take America's citizens far,
But by Jesus Christ's teaching and guidance America can become His shining star."

"And if we desire a land with His liberty and justice for all,
Let's trust our Savior Jesus, who died to free us from sin, arose again and lives to hear our
prayer-call."

Then at the train's jolt she awoke and found sad news on her iPad,
For it was a seminar by arrogant professors saying America's Christian past was mostly bad.

And true American history to these arrogant elites was mostly made-up and unknown,
So they just expressed faith in thought-diversity with a politically-correct tone.

But she wondered, will America's Christian leaders disappear like trains from their tracks,
For God-blessed precious history and heritage is sure under attack.

Then she prayed for wisdom, guidance and grace from above,
To tell her class how America's greatness and Constitution came through Christian love.

Moving On . . . Without Strife

But the Holy Spirit produces this kind of fruit in our lives: love, joy, peace, patience, kindness, goodness, faithfulness, gentleness, and self-control.

Galatians 5:22-23a NLT

It is wise to look back to the path from which one came,
And if strife has walked alongside, your future need not be the same.

For a new birth in Jesus can put you on a new purposeful road,
With God's Spirit as a companion in your earthly abode.

And if we don't ignore the Spirit's indwelling guidance to our soul,
Strife's companionship will depart as we let God's Spirit take control.

So Christian ... as you travel on, let the Spirit be your protective umbrella,
To keep you from turning back and being accompanied by that quarrelsome strife-fella.

But be filled with the Spirit.
Ephesians 5:18b NKJV

A Light for Your Path

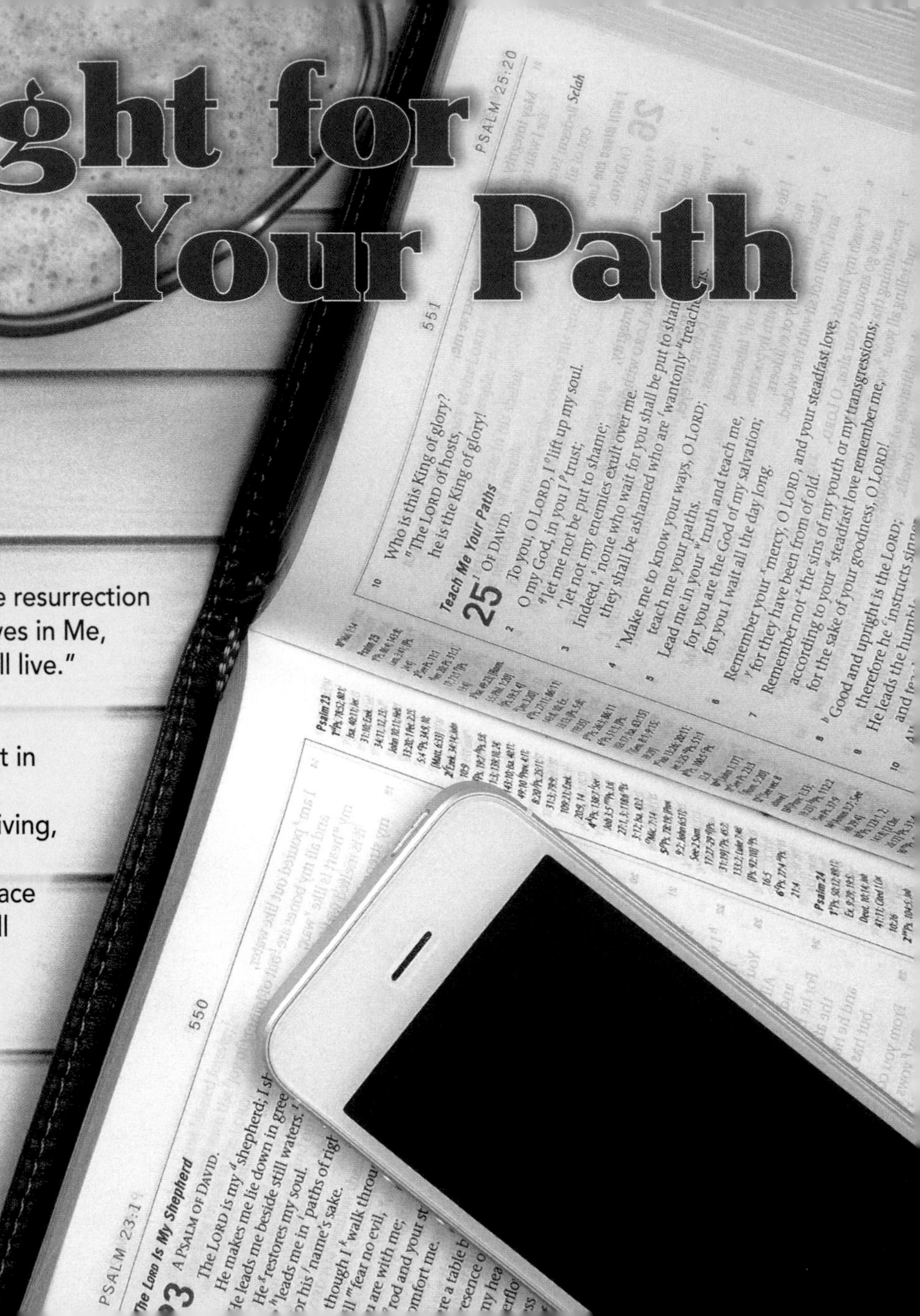

Jesus said to her, "I am the resurrection and the life. He who believes in Me, though he may die, he shall live."
John 11:25 NKJV

Be anxious for nothing, but in everything by prayer and supplication, with thanksgiving, let your requests be made known to God; and the peace of God, which surpasses all understanding, will guard your hearts and minds through Christ Jesus.
Philippians 4:6–7 NKJV

Your word *is* a lamp to my feet and a light to my path.
Psalm 119:105 NKJV

Is the great "I Am" at the top of your contact book?
And do you often call on Him or give His Word a look?

Or is your day filled with trivia from the internet and friends,
To where no prayer-time is left to Him to ascend?

For the cares of this world can soon get you down,
When you pick up worries and forget how God's love does abound.

But if you do put the Lord at the top of your friend-list,
Good perspective and peace all day may persist.

While you are happy about all your text contacts who tune in,
Be sure to make time for the Holy Spirit to work on your heart from within.

By keeping contact with the Savior at the top of your friend-list,
You will feel acceptance and experience true conversational bliss.

When seekers take troubles and cares directly to our Maker,
God promises peace and guidance to each willing partaker.

If your cell phone is blessed to hold a copy of God's Word,
The Book of Proverbs provides the greatest wisdom ever heard.

And a great thing about communication with our Omniscient Guide,
Is that we can be free of that controlling cell phone alongside.

Proverbs tells us of a Friend who sticks closer than a brother,
And time spent with the Lord will bear Spiritual fruit like no other.

So developing a habit of early fellowship with the Lord each day,
Can mute cellular gossip or despair and shoo pride away.

What a surprising blessing and witness to God's Amazing Grace,
To all those on your friends-list who may be seeking His face.

The UNMATCHED POWER of GOD'S Word

This morning I thought I will write something great which brings honor to Thee,
But I heard, "Dismiss that quest for it will bring pride ... not joy to thee."

And then The Spirit bid, "Just live your life controlled and empowered by Me,
For this is what a hungry audience can grasp and will rejoice to see."

I said, "I want to create a great poem, a picture, or a song,
To guide all those needy people to You, and help them along."

The Spirit whispered, "Salvation is by grace through faith in God's powerful Word,
And John 3:16 is the Gospel guideline which He wants all to have heard."

So I quit trying to bring God honor and glory through words which were clever,
And just put the emphasis on the Bible's clear words which proclaim the greatest *truth* ever.

"For God so loved the world that He gave His only begotten Son, that whoever believes in Him should not perish but have everlasting life."
John 3:16 NKJV

For the word of God is living and powerful, and sharper than a two-edged sword, piercing even to the division of the soul and spirit, and of joints and marrow, and is a discerner of the thoughts and intents of the heart.
Hebrews 4:12 NKJV

Playing the Fool

Whether in a Shakespearian play or real life, one can
"Play The Fool,"
But if it happens often in real life ... it ain't cool!

For folly which is amusing for a season will soon fade,
Or it may become a habit which in life may pervade.

And while people enjoy the circus act of a clown,
They avoid a perpetual fool whose antics wear them down.

So if you are blessed with the gift of humor and mirth,
Be sure it is prudent and never degrades a person's worth.

Laughter can be good when drawn from life or yourself,
But if it is harmful to others better put it on the shelf.

For cruel humor ill directed often boomerangs in the end,
And causes great harm to the jester like an unfaithful friend.

So use your humor to bring healthy laughter to lips,
But avoid unhealthy barbs which may destroy fellowships.

And the one folly-line which you must take care not to cross,
Is ill-humor about God which may bring hearers eternal loss.

For the Bible clearly tells where it is wise not to trod,
So don't "play the fool" and jest, "there is no God."

The fool has said in his heart, *"There is no God."*

Psalm 14:1 NKJV

The fear of the Lord *is* the beginning of knowledge, *but* fools despise wisdom and instruction.

Proverbs 1:7 NKJV

Walk with the wise and become wise, for a companion of fools suffers harm.

Proverbs 13:20 NIV

PRIDE'S DECEPTION

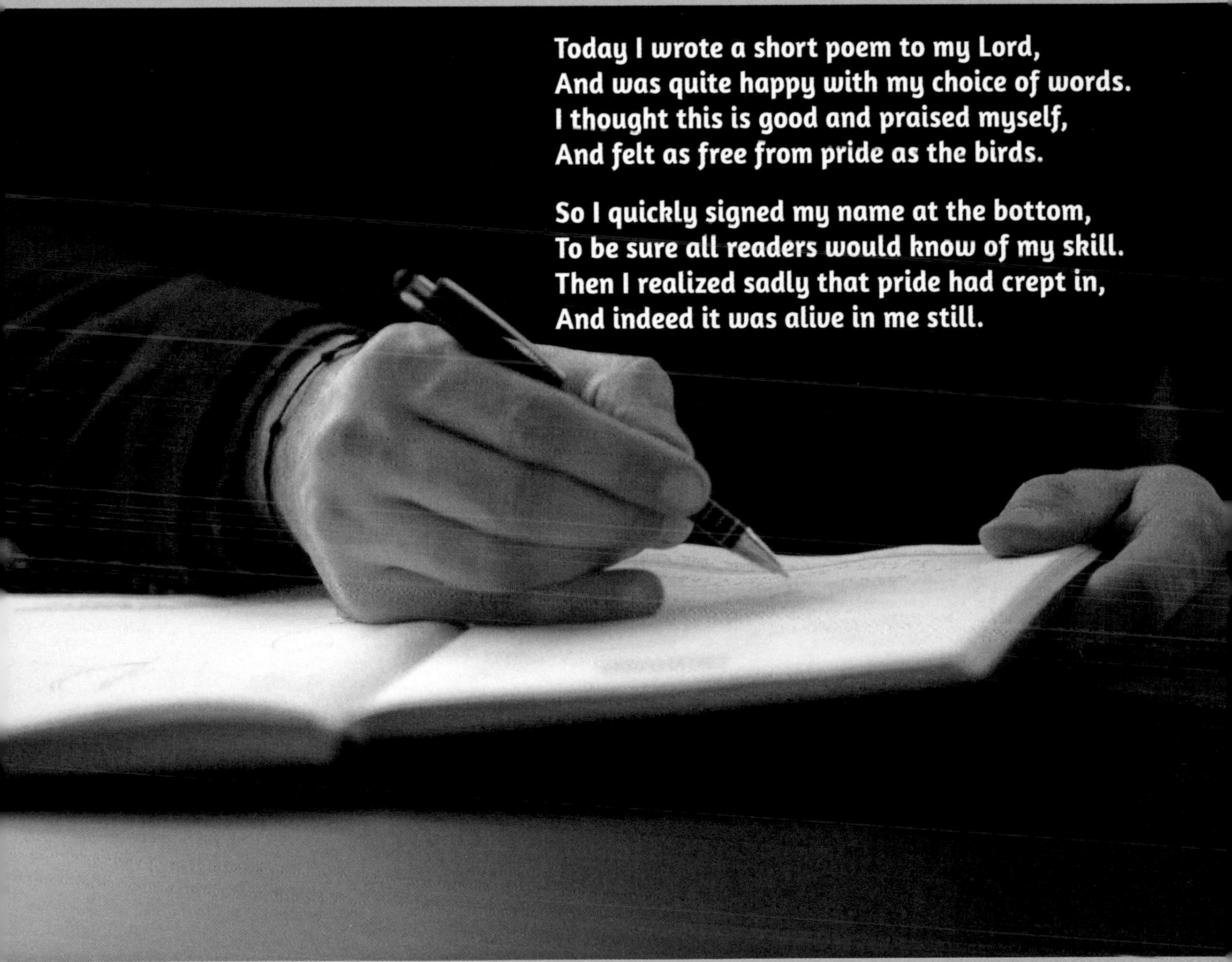

Today I wrote a short poem to my Lord,
And was quite happy with my choice of words.
I thought this is good and praised myself,
And felt as free from pride as the birds.

So I quickly signed my name at the bottom,
To be sure all readers would know of my skill.
Then I realized sadly that pride had crept in,
And indeed it was alive in me still.

Pride *goes* before destruction, and a haughty spirit before a fall.
Proverbs 16:18 NKJV

The Mirror's Guile

Who is that person looking back from the mirror on my wall?
And does she proclaim aloud, "You may be the fairest of them all"?

Did she just whisper, "You are quite remarkable you know,"
And cause me to forget the One who has made me so?

And does my mirror sing my praises as I turn away,
Causing me to forget I am merely God's piece of clay?

Then I wonder if I could pass through this mirror like Alice,
On the other side would I be seen as a queen fit for a palace?

Then I realize what appears on the left in my mirror is actually on the right,
The mirror's perspective is just the opposite from my earlier
day-dreaming delight.

So I slide my chair carefully to the left to see if this brings in anything new,
And noticed a Bible there which had been previously blocked from my view.

I realized my Soul's enemy was wanting me to leave my Bible behind,
And was leading my foolish imagination far from a rational, sound mind.

So I stopped talking to my reflection where the Bible was left out of sight,
And reached back to the right for my Bible for additional protection and insight.

I let my Bible fall open and picked a verse to recall: "Pride goes before
destruction and a haughty spirit before a fall."

And when I let my Bible pages take another tumble,
This verse read, "God resists the proud but gives grace to the humble."

"God resists the proud, but gives grace to the humble."
James 4:6b NKJV

Pride goes before destruction, a haughty spirit before a fall.
Proverbs 16:18 NIV

Text-Mate Awareness

Text-life can reduce real communication to a clever craft,
And sometimes it can make written words and pictures just an insincere draft.

For mere writing lacks the aid of sight, sound, and feel,
Plus these senses help one perceive what is real.

So keep your constant text contact from building a soundbite reality,
Which can develop a great hindrance to true relational vitality.

Or, when you meet your text-mate you may have little to say,
For elements like countenance and emotions have been hidden away.

A smile, a laugh, or body language can touch one's soul,
And provide and guide the affection and true respect which make a relationship whole.

So remember that text-life with a partner that gives you a thrill,
Should be vetted by face-to-face interaction revealing intellect, emotions, and will.

What is put into a text can too easily be misread on another's mind-screen,
And later have sad consequences which were quite unforeseen.

So be aware that text communication may be only twenty percent true,
In revealing the true heart and soul of a text-partner to you.

Remember Bible reading and prayer can keep you on an even keel,
While providing wisdom and guidance for perceiving what is phony and what is real.

Keep your heart with all diligence,
for out of it *spring* the issues of life.

Proverbs 4:23 NKJK

Grasping the Important

True beauty often evades the eye of the beholder,
And earlier cares and concerns may prove robbers when we grow older.

My Sunshine Sue and I took a walk across a meadow green,
Soon golden dandelions were mixed into this gorgeous scene.

My daughter picked a bouquet of blossoms she wanted me to see,
But I was deep in thought on when our next yard spray should be.

A voice in my soul said, "Enjoy this gift which I prepared for you,"
And suddenly weeds shone like flowers in the face of my Sunshine Sue.

Down the trail a few dandelion heads had already turned to white,
I thought those white balls in my yard would surely be a bad site.

But Sue's face was aglow as she gave me her bouquet of fun,
And as she blew, seeds parachuted down a bright beam of the sun.

The Voice again pled, "Enjoy this time-treasure with Sue today,
And just let the cares of this world like bad seeds blow away."

By God's grace, years later as I sit in my room all alone,
Sweet memories abide of that day as I wait to go home.

But the vision of that day with my Sunshine Sue still shines bright,
While troubling thoughts about dandelions are nowhere in sight.

Now I await my Sunshine Sue with grandkids to
    brighten my way,
And I thank God's Spirit for whispering to me
    through His dandelions that day.

The earth ***is*** *the Lord's, and all its fullness, The world and those who dwell therein.*
Psalm 24:1 NKJV

Old-Timer's Rhyme

Some people ask, "Richard, why do you write rhyme?"
Well, now in my eighties, I find plenty of slack time.

For while my mind moves slower to pick up the past,
Finding just the right words helps fond memories to last.

And if my thoughts are tied closely to wisdom from the Bible,
I find it brings peace and a sense of personal revival.

God is not through with us while living on earth,
And Bible blessings extend to old age all the way from birth.

So rhyme is a pastime to challenge my brain,
As it takes me back down that old memory lane.

And it doesn't matter if my stuff to others is profound,
It's just my way of keeping happy memories around.

True, life's short journey is filled with happiness and pain,
But God's Word assures that in heaven all will be gain.

For our Savior bought us out of the "slave market of sin,"
So life above could continue with all who love Him.

Now many Bible promises locked in my brain,
Comfort my soul as I await heaven's train.

And I pray that old-timers who read my rhyme,
Craft their own happy poems to bless their remaining lifetime.

Being confident of this very thing, that He who has begun a good work in you will complete *it* until the day of Jesus Christ.

Philippians 1:6 NKJV

The Power of Kind Words

> *"In the same way, let your light shine before others, that they may see your good deeds and glorify your Father in heaven."*
>
> *Matthew 5:16 NIV*

Will we walk through life with nothing to say?
With a frown on our face which turns people away?

For the ray of sunshine that is yours to share,
May lift someone's spirits from a world of care.

A happy greeting can make one feel whole,
And go right to a heart and lift up one's soul.

It can say, "Hey, you really matter", and help one to see,
An attitude adjustment could be a blessing to me.

Look for small things you can sincerely compliment,
For blessings like these can appear angel-sent.

And when we connect with nice things seldom heard,
It can bring a smile to one's face, for your kind words.

And a "Thank you for your smile"
can brighten things more,
To where they perceive God's knock
on their heart's door.

The wonderful Gospel comes
through saints who care,
And seek God's divine appoint-
ments and then take time to share.

Remembering My Day-Maker

Wow! God has given me another day to behold,
But what it may bring I have not been told.

Now I have great plans and my hopes are sky-high,
But for all I know, this could be the very day I die.

No precious day can be bought or sold,
And its worth in advance we are never told.

So when success seems sure as I chart my day,
I'm aware, the best plans of men oft do go astray.

I have purpose to greet each day with joy, hope, and love,
And to dismiss bad thoughts and grasp God's help from above.

I recall man's plans which seemed headed for adversity,
But then turned into blessings by God's creative diversity.

So when I awake not knowing what this new day may hold,
By God's grace, may the Day-Maker keep my Christian faith bold!

This *is* the day the Lord has made; we will rejoice and be glad in it.

Psalms 118:24 NKJV

The Fish's Sermon

The water lay still and so quiet,
For the wind and waves were at peace.

I cast my lure to the rocky shore,
And fishing gave my life a new lease.

Business challenges had faded far away,
Filed in my memory bank for another day.

The trees' reflection enchanted the water below,
As they tried to influence where my bait should go.

My reel sang softly spinning line to my bait in the air,
And I whispered thanks for the time of escape from all care.

But as my lure touched the water close by the shore,
An explosion occurred as a big fish with my bait did soar.

My heart skipped a beat when I viewed the length of the fish,
I thought "This one's for my wall and will not go on a dish."

My hope was shattered as the fish again took to the air,
And shook the bait from his mouth and right into my hair.

For a moment disappointment ruled my soul,
Till a smile crossed my face and I laid down my pole.

And my thoughts of conquest and a mount on my wall,
Turned to praise God, the blessed Creator of it all.

My mind thought of Jesus and the Bible again,
And I was reminded how Jesus had said, "Go fish for the souls of men!"

After a pause to marvel this fish's masterful rejection,
I had to smile again at my soul's Biblical selection.

Then He said to them, "Follow Me, and I will make you fishers of men."
Matthew 4:19 NKJV

The Winning Attitude

The day was superb as we headed out onto the lake,
And I was thankful for each cast we would soon take.

Bob and Sam were to join me for a fishing thrill,
Both men had applied for the same job at our mill.

I stopped by the dock to pick up the two men,
And headed out for an angling adventure
once again.

The waves always seemed happy to have us afloat,
As they played their percussion on the side of
my boat.

Bob smiled ear to ear as the waves hit the side,
But Sam seemed to be aggravated with the
rough ride.

The water was smooth at our first fishing spot,
But Sam's line got tangled up and boy was he hot!

Bob yelled and water boiled as the first big fish bit;
Sam grumbled and was upset that Bob got the
first hit.

The fish in my net scrambled our gear all about;
I was thrilled with Bob's catch but Sam began to pout.

As we took time for some pictures, Sam's anger exploded;
He drank more from his flask and continued to get loaded.

Weeds seemed to attack Sam's lure most of the day,
And he cursed when he had to clean them away.

For Sam the boat was always too close or far from the shore;
Bob and I just calmly fished and caught more and more.

When we ran to an island for a shore lunch of fried fish,
We discovered Sam was a vegan and passed on this dish.

Bob quickly gathered the wood while I cut the filets,
And Sam retreated to the boat to keep bears away.

Thunder in the distance caused Sam again to complain;
Bob said, "I hear fish bite well before a storm and the rain."

The storm was not bad and while Sam sat drinking a beer,
I cleaned up the camp as Bob loaded the boat with our gear.

We had our limit of fish to take back to the camp,
Even Sam caught a few as he complained of being damp.

Bob whistled as we cleaned a mountain of fish that day,
But Sam was off to the lodge and never came back our way.

Bob gave me a high five when we finally stood still,
And I knew I'd found a great fit to work at the mill.

I recalled my father's counsel as our work was all done.

"If you want to learn about a man, just go fish with him, son!"

And as I thought of Jesus' times with his disciples and fish,
I thanked God for our day and Dad's counsel on my selection wish.

This is the day which the Lord hath made; we will rejoice and be glad in it.

Psalms 118:24 KJV

Evening Bliss in a North Woods

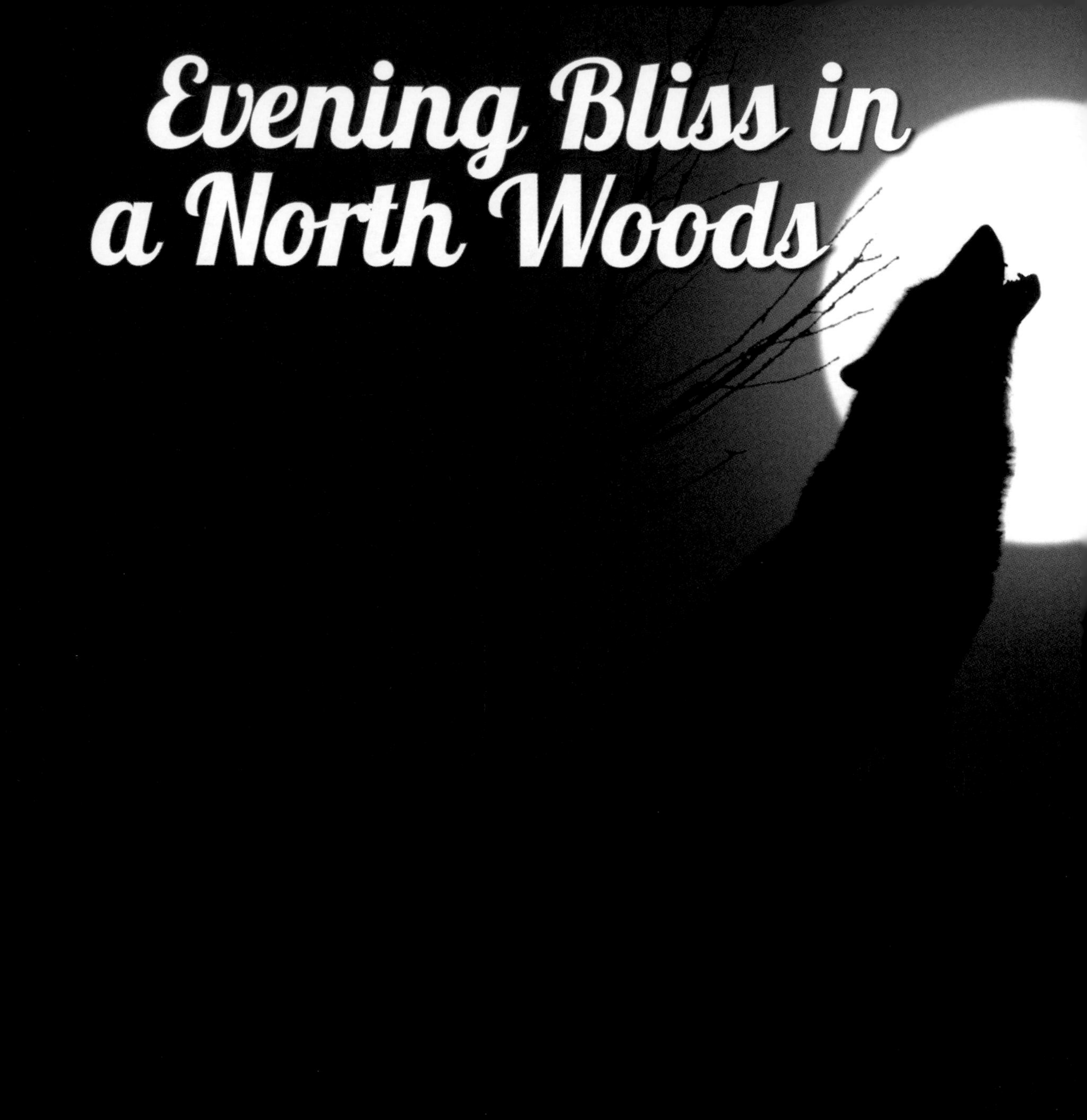

Have you gazed at a full moon as it spreads its soft light,
Across God's landscape and lake as it welcomed the night?

Then put out your campfire and hung up your gear,
And crawled into your sleeping bag ... a serenade to hear.

Hearing the loons' mournful call float across a sparkling lake,
Letting their family know it was time for the night rest they should take.

Then hearing the mighty eagles give forth their unimpressive last squall,
All nested up in a damaged pine which is the tallest of them all.

And felt the low vibrating beats of an owl's plaintiff hoot,
Echoed by his friend whose call will exactly follow suit.

In prayer praised God for this kind wilderness revelation,
As you felt His great love for you in His awesome creation.

Then as if to keep the birds from stealing God's nighttime show.
You heard the wolves add in their howling as off to sweet dreams you did go.

**You will keep *him* in perfect peace,
Whose mind *is* stayed on *You*.**

Isaiah 26:3a NKJV

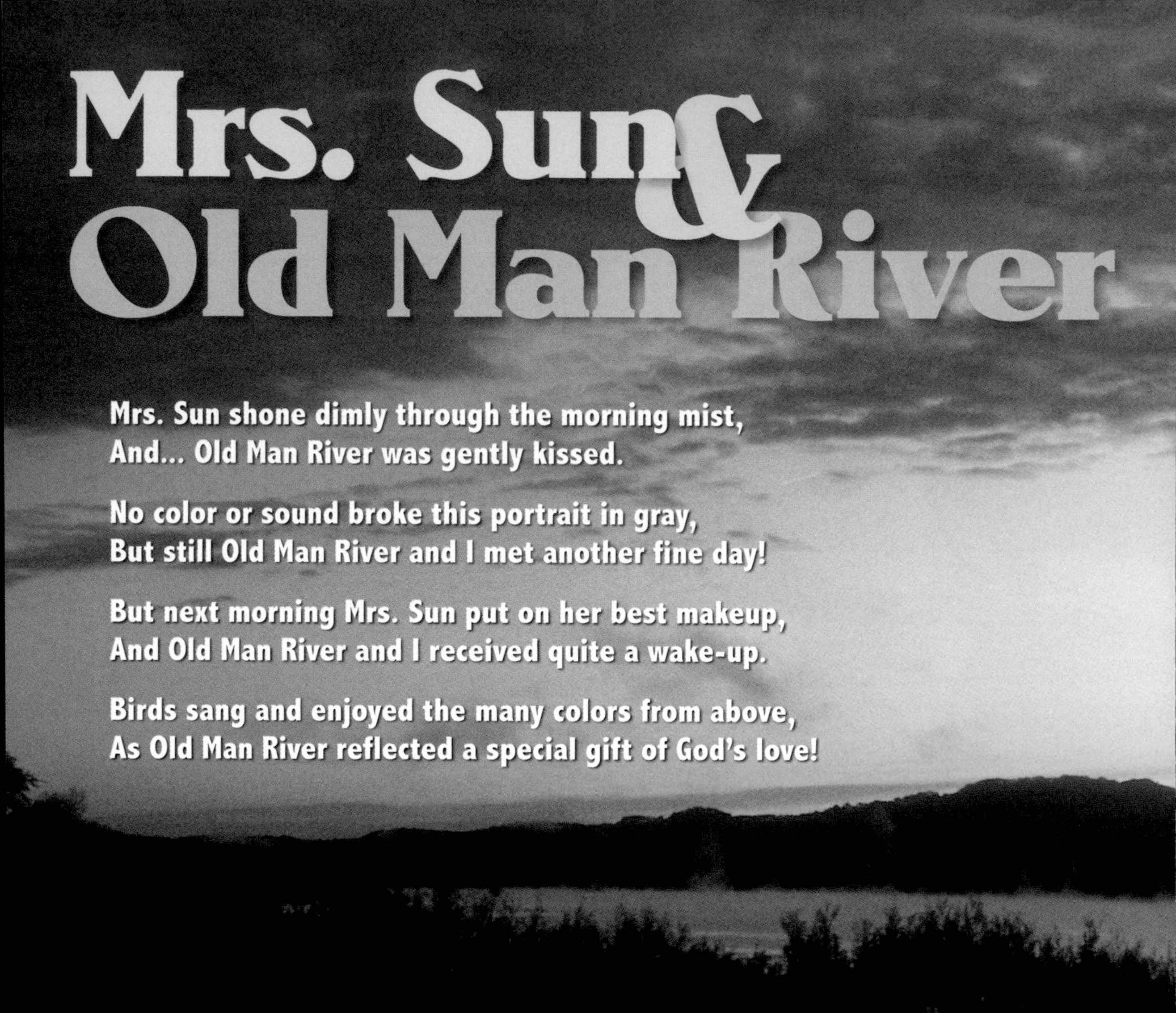

Mrs. Sun & Old Man River

Mrs. Sun shone dimly through the morning mist,
And... Old Man River was gently kissed.

No color or sound broke this portrait in gray,
But still Old Man River and I met another fine day!

But next morning Mrs. Sun put on her best makeup,
And Old Man River and I received quite a wake-up.

Birds sang and enjoyed the many colors from above,
As Old Man River reflected a special gift of God's love!

From the rising of the sun to its going down, the Lord's name *is* to be praised.
Psalm 113:3 NKJV

Sea Gulls

When the dove returned to him (Noah) in the evening, there in its beak was a freshly plucked olive leaf!

Genesis 8:11 NIV

I wish I could fly like graceful birds up above,
Gliding through the air with songs that I love.

And give out a sweet twill like mocking birds do,
To bring encouragement to listeners like me
and you.

But I would not like to be a seagull, so noisy
and brash,
With squawks and complaints as it picks up trash.

Disrupting the peace of a day on the beach,
As they fight with each other over anything to eat.

Now they are beautiful when soaring way up
in the sky,
And I know God put them here with a good
reason why.

I just wish they would do their noisy garbage run,
When I was not on the beach drinking up the sun.

I prefer the peaceful coo of a gentle dove,
As I know Noah did when it announced God's
salvation from above.

God's Amazing Pine Trees

The heavens declare the glory of God,
and the firmament shows His handiwork.
Psalm 19:1 NKJV

What magnificent lakes God's glaciers have carved out in the North,
And in Canada, more lakes than in all other lands have come forth.

God's ice-bulldozers carved shorelines of rock, hills and walls,
And created the small feeding streams and roaring waterfalls.

Then God decorated the rock shorelines with beautiful ponderosa and white pine,
Though their roots seem to have no soil upon which to dine.

But still, some hold fast to the rocks and grow to a great height,
And lean over the water at angles which would give an engineer fright.

Their root system holds fast through so many a storm,
Till old age or calamity causes this anchor's failure to perform.

If you're blessed to fish a shoreline into which one of these trees took a fall.
Take care, for this water-structure may hide the biggest fish of them all!

The Cat's Meow

I awoke to my cat's meow, "Pay attention to me!"
So I slipped out of bed to see what her demand could be.

Was I late for her morning bowl of milk or cream?
Or did she just resent my lingering over a sweet dream?

She quickly deposited a gift in her messy litter box,
To avoid the rain and cold outside, like a clever old fox.

When I sat down for breakfast, she purred round my feet,
Till I got up for my morning toast, and she took over my seat.

She demanded I pet her by a progressive bite on my hand,
As she purred a love-song to herself and drifted off to cat dream-land.

My nose itched as I brushed her and cleaned up cat hair,
While her smiling meows said, "What a great life we share."

And when I left for my car, her meow seemed to say,
"Buy only the best cat food when you go shopping today."

When I glanced back at her haughty air by the door,
It said, "Hurry back soon so you can work for me more."

Then the covert meaning of her parting meow did land,
"What a fine house and servant now meet my every wish and demand!"

Have dominion over the fish of the sea,
over the birds of the air, and over every
living thing that moves on the earth.

Genesis 1:28b NKJV

EXERCISE TODAY?

"I think I shall go take a walk," I proclaimed from my bed this morning,
But my body protested, "Hey I'm tired, I need more warning."

Then I pulled up the covers and procrastination bid, "Snuggle in tight,
You can always go for a walk! Go at noon or maybe tonight."

Around lunchtime a reminder drifted down from my brain,
And said, "Couldn't you go run now and skip eating again?"

But my appetite was already planning on a fine meal of pancakes and eggs,
And my taste buds proclaimed, "Eat-up! You need energy for your weary legs."

As evening approached, I was looking for my walking shoes,
When my ears heard the TV announce, "There's much to report in the evening news."

I paused then to ponder what in the world could have happened today,
And curiosity said, "Better listen to what Mr. Know-it-all has to say."

It seemed but a moment when my watch announced it's time for dinner,
And my nose told me, "This one smells like a culinary winner."

As I dug into a fine meal, my mind questioned "Hey, who is the Captain of this ship?"
Then I prayed to God my Almighty Captain for willpower and His enabling fellowship.

And now even the clock and the scale seemed to proclaim 'Amen' to a walk,
So I laced up my shoes and headed out for a prayer walk and talk.

After walking a block, my senses were back in the exercise game,
As I passed great walking sights, new sounds and good feelings flooded my brain.

And I praised my Captain for canceling out thoughts which to me were discouraging,
And replacing them with needed willpower and His joyful encouraging.

I remembered then, "You have not because you ask not," is proclaimed in God's word,
And I thanked Him that my request for joyful exercise was a prayer the Almighty
had heard.

I can do all things through
Christ who strengthens me.

Philippians 4:13 (NKJV)

A BY-FAITH ATTITUDE

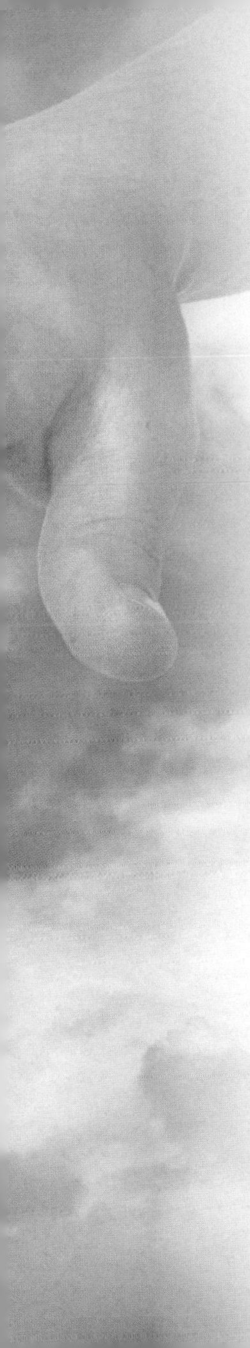

What miracles occur when a positive attitude prevails?
For it shoos gloom away when doubt and fear assails.

But when someone shares an idea which excites their heart,
It is often killed by a frown, a laugh, or a sneer at the start.

And as you look back at wild ideas which are great products today,
You see they were once just silly proposals which doubters cast away.

Whether it's a cell phone, television, or the car you travel in today,
They were once, "Impossible!" .... the unbelievers did say.

God never ceases to surprise us from His vast innovation store,
And grants amazing inventions to those who open by faith His Possibility Door.

Many innovations and services which were but dreams a few years ago,
Have sparked huge new technologies which are now on the grow.

So why should we doubt God's by-faith promises to you and me,
When man's once by-faith imaginations are now all around us to see?

For while God's omniscience will grant knowledge while our bodies turn to dust,
He has promised we'll be with Him forever, if by faith in His Son Jesus we trust.

And the Bible reveals God's by-faith path to everlasting life,
For Jesus assures us, "I am the way, the truth, and the life."

So above all, keep a positive by-faith attitude toward God and His Word,
And it will anchor your heart with the best news ever heard.

So then faith *comes* by hearing, and hearing by the word of God.
Romans 10:17 NKJV

But without faith *it is* impossible to please *Him*.
Hebrews 11:6a NKJV

Truth

"There is no such thing as truth," said the professor to the class,
And all sat still except one normally quiet lass.

She raised her hand bravely to pose a question,
But was ignored by the prof who welcomed no suggestion.

The prof carried on with a gleeful smile,
"Now let's think about this for awhile."

"Truth can't be absolute. No wise person would believe that,
For what is true for me may be as certain as fact.

While what you perceive to be true to the core,
For me might be merely a ridiculous bore.

So you see no one wise would believe truth is sure,
For to believe that would be a puzzlement
without a cure."

As the professor turned, the young lady was now
on her feet,
And he acknowledged her question and said,
"Now take your seat."

"Now what is the problem which disturbs your soul?
If you tell us please, it may make us all whole."

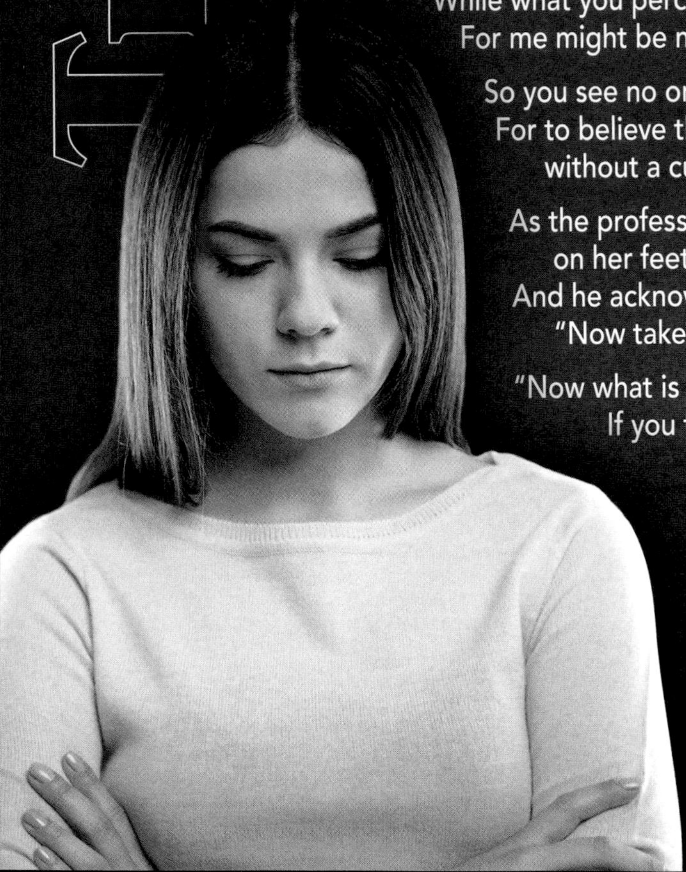

Many in the class had a laugh at the prof's wit,
But it soon stopped as she with tears agreed to sit.

She said, "My problem is with your premise that there is no truth,
For how can this statement be true, if there is no truth?"

"You can see why my faith in your statement is in doubt,
For my faith is placed in another Teacher who turned
my life about."

"And who is this more knowledgeable professor
than I?" said he.
"The One who declared, I am the way, the truth
and the life!" said she.

Then the class grew quiet and many expressions
showed change,
Some to love, some to anger and some desiring a
life rearrange.

But all left impacted by the lesson that day,
And they say even the professor began
to pray.

Jesus said to him, "I am the way, the truth and the life. No one comes to the Father except through Me."

John 14:6 NKJV

Christmas Future

My sheep hear My voice, and I know them, and they follow Me. And I give them eternal life, and they shall never perish.

John10:27-28a NKJV

I and *My* Father are one.

John 10:30 NKJV

Oh the joys of "Christmas Past" with our parents and old friends dear,
Come back as fondest memories when the carols reach our ear.

Soon our kids and grandkids will plan to celebrate with us here,
And we plan to build sweet memories for them also to hold dear.

Bygone years have been so kind, and our health is still OK,
Though our steps have begun to slow as we traverse along life's way.

And as our souls rejoice for the great gift of those sweet "Christmas Past,"
The days and family players flow together into one timeless cast.

And while the folk lore of Santa and Frosty blow away like a snowy dream,
The Truth of the precious Christ Child shines a bright eternal beam.

And while the bells sing out our Salvation through the birth of God's only Son,
Our great hope is to praise Jesus eternally when our lives on earth are done!

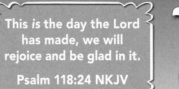

A Country Boy's Creed

This *is* the day the Lord has made, we will rejoice and be glad in it.

Psalm 118:24 NKJV

When cares of this world knock at my tractor door,
I shall reply, "Go away, I'm not here for you anymore!"

For God's Spirit and Word did bid my heart, "Be still!
Don't let those foolish invaders turn you from My Will.

But let the Seed of My Word touch your heart each day,
Like the sweet aroma from this field of new-mown hay.

For foolish worries sure detour your mind from My Will,
Like the stupor from drinking from that old moonshine still."

So this Country Boy now discards worry in a New York minute,
As I thank God for each farm day and rejoice mightily in it.

A NORTH WOODS' STORM

He calms the storm, so that its waves are still.

Psalm 107:29 NKJV

So the men marveled, saying, "Who can this be, that even the winds and sea obey Him."

Matthew 8:27b NKJV

I love to fall asleep in a North Woods' storm,
When all the elements of nature are ready to perform.

And if blessed to be in an old island cabin out on a lake,
When I trim my lantern at night, I can't long stay awake.

The moon outside my window casts her silver path across still waters,
While loons give a soothing call to their baby sons and small daughters.

While my sleepy prayers arise to God in grateful delight,
My ears hear a low rumble far off into the night.

My mind drifts away to storms I have enjoyed fishing in before,
Where strong winds whistled through the pines and big waves broke upon
the shore.

When a crash disrupts a dream of my boat upon a rock,
I awaken with a start to hear my boat bumping against the dock.

This storm is real as lightning flashes and thunder echoes like a war,
And soon rain upon the roof mimics a waterfall's loud roar.

As lightning strikes a nearby tree, electricity fills the air,
And I wonder just how many people this old cabin has sheltered there.

Soon the rain dies down to a light pitter-patter on the roof,
As the quick moving storm now leaves me totally aloof.

Now sparkling waters and a starry sky present an awesome peace outside,
And I recall God's faithful promise to be my storm shelter and true guide.

I gaze at the heavens of the clear northern sky,
A billion stars do praise Him, and a goodnight meteor streaks by.

Now as the loons repeat their soothing all's well lullaby,
I snuggle back down in my bunk, with a deep contented sigh.

Loonie
Toonies

I love the way that a loon gently nurtures her chicks,
And has them ride on her back and teaches them how to catch fish.

And while loons can't use words like humans and all,
They do communicate with each other by their amazing bird call.

Their calls may guide each other when flying up high over a bay,
Or down on water to warn their chicks of a boat or an angler's bait coming their way.

Loons do seem to enjoy still fishermen and often pop up next to their boat,
Which confirms there are fish below, so watch to be sure your cork is afloat.

And what a thrill when a loon's call echoes back and forth off a rock wall,
As if they are laughing at their duck friends whose quacks can't echo at all.

Then when evening darkness begins to fall across the bay,
Loons may give out a long soothing call to end a fine fishing day.

Sometimes late in the night you may awaken to the craziest commotion of all,
As the loons seem to be drunk and holding a wild nighttime ball.

Those wild parties may have birthed the saying, "as crazy as a loon,"
I am sure thankful that God blessed my ears to hear their unique loonie tune.

How many are your works, Lord! In wisdom you made them all; the earth is full of your creatures.

Psalm 104:24 NIV

A Lake's Changing Face

"An excellent wife *is* the crown of her husband."
Proverbs 12:4a NKJV

The lake had a thousand islands and many a bay,
And the cabin we rented was the only place to stay.

I had assured my wife we would enjoy this remote place,
And she accepted the challenge, but with doubt on her face.

Now when on a lake with a thousand islands at night,
The moon and wind can hide changing a previous sight.

But that morning my small outboard sang a happy song,
And I glanced back for sure waypoints as my boat sped along.

Big waves slapped the side of my wee fishing boat,
As I tacked across a rough bay to stay safely afloat.

Fishing looked good out of the wind over there,
So I headed across the wide bay with nary a care.

I gripped the motor's handle as the spray washed my face,
Excited to captain my ship to this new fishing place.

Ah, my decision was good for I found an abundance of fish,
And this fine catch of walleye would fill many a dish.

But as I reeled-up my last fish, a battle did loom,
For a muskie also wanted this fish to consume.

My heart pounded as I scrambled for my casting gear,
With a vision of catching a big muskie this year.

I ignored the sun's glow now fading in the west,
I lay down long casts which were my absolute best.

I tried every great lure and angling trick in the books,
But this muskie just teased me with follow-up looks.

And as darkness dismissed this cat-and-mouse game,
Day turned into night and nothing looked the same.

So I headed home looking for waypoints and familiar sights,
As a full moon peaked through the clouds, much to my delight.

Still the reflection of tall pines on the rock hills and the shore,
Made distances on the calm lake look smaller than before.

And questionable key waypoints now all seemed to lie,
As glances back often failed as we passed on by.

My prayer life improved passing over many a rock reef and weed bed,
Hoping for enough gas to cover the distance wrong waypoints may have led.

I paused to look at a place to possibly spend the night on shore,
But wolves howled and I saw a bear as the boat eased in more.

But after many doubts about my dead reckoning most of the way,
I finally rounded the last bend to a light flickering down the end of the bay.

I received a hug and apologized for worrying my sweet wife so,
But must confess my wild adventure like the muskie's size did grow.

THE FAST FOOD LESSON

Two burger flippers worked side by side,
One seemed happy; the other dissatisfied.

Joe smiled like a great chef preparing a fine steak,
But Jim pitched meat on a grill with a scowl on his face.

Joe envisioned the patron his culinary delight would bless,
While Jim just complained, scraping off his over-cooked mess.

Joe hummed a tune which matched the joy in his heart,
As Jim verbalized, "For this job I'm much too smart."

Both men desired prosperity and to gain more pay,
And both hoped a great new job would come their way.

Well the restaurant's owner came looking for a partner one day,
And guess at whose door opportunity knocked and offered great pay?

For Joe learned the best way to bide time while pursuing a dream,
Was to do an excellent job right there while moving upstream.

And Jim also had some learning to do,
For a slack job reputation follows after you.

And whatever you do, do it heartily, as to the Lord and not to men.

Colossians 3:23 NKJV

Do you see a man *who* excels in his work? He will stand before kings.

Proverbs 22:29 NKJV

Four Great Friends

Dad encouraged me to know Mr. Protective Instinct and Mr. Presence of Mind,
For they walk hand-in-hand together and are two faithful friends of a kind.

Dad said if I make their acquaintance early in life,
They will spare me much pain and unnecessary strife.

But there were two other friends Dad also urged me to know well,
He said the great value of befriending both Mr. Wisdom and Mr. Common Sense
would take eternity to tell.

Though I often strayed from hanging out with these True Friends,
My dad's counsel and their guidance swung me back to home-base again.

Now I have learned what caused my father to be so wise,
These Four Great Friends walk the pages of Proverbs to open blind eyes.

The fear of the Lord *is* the beginning of wisdom.
Psalms 111:10 NKJV

A prudent person foresees danger and takes precautions. The simpleton goes blindly on and suffers the consequences.
Proverbs 27:12 NLT

Good judgment wins favor, but the way of the unfaithful leads to their destruction.
Proverbs 13:15 NIV

Sunrise Sunset

Today I awoke to a beautiful sunrise reflecting on a calm North Woods' lake,
My heart filled with thanksgiving as questions in my mind did awake.

Why should I be greeted with such a display of God's creative glory?
Could it be to bring joy for what's to be written today in my life story?

Then I watched the colors change and fade as clouds now hid the great view,
But His spirit reminded me, "When clouds come, I'm always there for you."

I headed out for a great fishing day and to enjoy the beauty of this land,
Then as evening arrived I was blessed by a double header as an awesome sunset did expand.

Later in bed I pondered, "Could any day have a better beginning or end than this?"
Then His presence seemed to whisper, "Wait until you experience my heavenly bliss."

The Lord has done it this very day; let us rejoice today and be glad.
Psalm 118:24 NIV

A QUEST FULFILLED

I pondered, "Where can I find real peace and guidance this day?"
And God's Spirit whispered, "Let me show your heart the way."

Then my wandering eye fixed on a dusty Bible on my shelf,
And I thought, "Can I understand that profound book all by myself?"

I thumbed through and by chance stopped at Proverbs, Chapter One,
To find a clue about why my mind seemed so undone.

Verse One read, "Fear of the Lord is the beginning of wisdom,"
And as I thought about wisdom, I knew I did lack some.

So I turned to a Bible verse a friend once book-marked for me,
And it said, "Spiritual wisdom and understanding to a natural man
cannot be."

This friend had also marked the Gospel of John, Chapter Three,
Where a Born-Again leader had for Jesus the same life-questions as me.

My heart was warmed as my quest ended at John Three, Verse Sixteen,
For I found peace there reading the greatest news ever seen.

Then I read all of John's Gospel and marveled how such amazing Grace could be.
As the warmth of God's love and acceptance became real for me.

Now I can't wait to explore the rest of the Bible,
For friends say thousands of promises insure my soul's everlasting survival.

But the natural man does not receive the things of the Spirit of God, for they are foolishness to him; nor can he know *them,* because they are spiritually discerned.

1 Corinthians 2:14 NKJV

"I am the way, the truth, and the life. No one comes to the Father except through Me."

John 14:6b NKJV

"For God so loved the world that He gave His only begotten Son, that whoever believes in Him should not perish but have everlasting life."

John 3:16 NKJV

THOSE BIG DOCTRINAL WORDS

You say He is omnipotent, well what does that mean?
It means He is all powerful and can bless your life dream.

You say He is omniscient, but what is that to me?
God loves and cares for you and caused all creation to be.

You say He is omnipresent, is that a good thing for us all?
Yes, He holds the universe together and still hears our every call.

You say He is perfectly righteous, but what about my sin?
He is altogether good and can grant you a new birth within.

You say His Love is unconditional, even if my love has worn thin.
Ah, but He is rich in grace and mercy and can take away that sin.

You say He is immutable, why is that important for me to know?
His attributes never change like our feelings which come and go.

You say His life is eternal, but why should that matter to me?
Since God has no beginning or end, in heaven we may forever be.

So how can I know this Prime Mover of whom you lovingly speak?
Rejoice, for His Son Jesus has given the key to what our hearts seek.

For by the sacrifice and resurrection of God's Son Jesus, freedom has been won,
And if we accept His Saving Grace by faith, the "Eternal Life Contract" is done.

And John 3:16 in the Bible becomes a guarantee on God's part,
And belief by repentant souls will give them a brand new heart.

For by faith they replace the "whoever" and put their own name therein,
And become a new spiritual creature, set free from "the slave market of sin."

"For God so loved the world that he gave his one and only Son, that whoever believes in him shall not perish but have eternal life."

John 3:16 NIV

Walking Unaware

Beware of the Florida swamp where the gators hang around,

For if you fail to pay attention you could be the next creature to go down.

For if one meanders along observing only the birds and the bees,

One may overlook an old log or what is hiding behind the trees.

And if it is dusk, you may catch a flash of the gleam in the gator's eye,

But if he is hungry, you won't even have time to whisper good-bye.

So keep your wits about you with eyes upon the ground,

If you wander the Everglades where the gators hang around.

There's an even greater danger lurking at our heart's door,

That old serpent (satan) wants to capture a soul even more.

For he leads the proud astray with clever ploys to confuse and conceal the door,

To a simple faith in Jesus as Savior for abundant life here and evermore.

Now the serpent was more cunning than any beast of the field which the Lord God had made.

Genesis 3:1 NKJV

"I am the door. If anyone enters by Me, he will be saved and will go in and out and find pasture."

John 10:9 NKJV

"My sheep hear My voice, and I know them, and they follow Me. And I give them eternal life, and they shall never perish; neither shall anyone snatch them out of My hand."

John 10:27- 28 NKJV

So they said, "Believe on the Lord Jesus Christ, and you will be saved, you and your household."

Acts 16:31 NKJV

Casting all your care upon Him, for He cares for you. Be sober, be vigilant; because your adversary the devil walks about like a roaring lion, seeking whom he may devour.

1 Peter 5:7-8 NKJV

Servant Leadership

I was asked to explain servant leadership today,
And how it could bless a business in an operational way.

I had to admit that servant leadership did not come naturally to me,
And that no by-the-book leadership training had caused this to be.

Now the aim of successful companies is to serve the customers
they sell,
But to make this really happen, their own business people must
serve each other well.

This can't happen in a "dog-eat-dog" business plight,
For even a great mission and core values can't make business people
serve right.

While wise documents are sure vital, they only better help us to see,
That only God's love and grace can motivate servant leadership
to be.

While sound policies and procedures are vital to maintain a sound enterprise,
It is how these guidelines are voiced and carried out that makes them when practiced wise.

When a top leader's heart sees fellow workers as people whom God loves,
Kind acts and communication flow down like spiritual oil from above.

For Jesus told us clearly what servant leaders must do,
When he simply told us, "Do to others as you would have them do to you."

And God's servant leadership love can flow back up from the lowest position in the shop,
When golden rule love has flown down with grace and kindness from the top.

When leadership directives must flow down on a business subject that's tough,
Golden rule servant leadership can return back up with more love and teamwork than enough.

"Do to others as you would have them do to you."

Luke 6:31 NIV

"So in everything, do to others what you would have them do to you, for this sums up the Law of the Prophets."

Matthew 7:12 NIV

And He sat down, called the twelve, and said to them, "If anyone desires to be first, he shall be last of all and servant of all."

Mark 9:35 NKJV

A Prudent Pause

There is a good reason for the yellow in a stop-and-go light,
For this reminder is to look both ways to avoid one's worst fright.

But do we ignore a guiding light and the alarm God has provided
to our being,
Which gives a warning to all when our speech may bring great harm
unforeseen?

Statements or reactions disregarding how others may reason,
Can cause relational problems which may plague us for many a
tough season.

For help to perceive when our speech should go on or just rest,
Send up a short prayer for the kind words and actions which are best.

If one's mind is preloaded with Biblical knowledge,
You may perceive a wiser response than ever learned in college.

For God has promised His Holy Spirit can bring joy to our lips and soul,
And supply the gifts of kindness, goodness, and self-control.

So why not install a yellow reminder-light in your mind,
Which activates a prayer request to be perceptive, gracious, and kind?

But the Holy Spirit produces this kind of fruit in our lives: love, joy, peace, patience, kindness, goodness, faithfulness, gentleness, and self-control.

Galatians 5:22-23a NLT

The Christian's Bar of Soap

My sin bothered me greatly and affected my sleep at night,
And the thought that it was known in heaven was a fright.

Then I opened my Bible to the only verse I really knew,
And the wonderful truth of John 3:16 came into view.

And while I clung to this promise with all my belief,
Something still bothered me and I felt little relief.

Then my hand thumbed Bible pages to another book that John wrote,
And the words in the first chapter were a welcome lifeboat.

For I found a "bar of soap" as I read 1 John 1:9,
And by faith I washed with it, till forgiveness became mine.

And when I arose from my knees, I was breathing fresh air,
For God gave me a right Spirit and I was freed from sin's snare.

If we confess our sins, He is faithful and just to forgive us *our* sins and to cleanse us from all unrighteousness.

1 John 1:9 NKJV

Create in me a clean heart, O God, and renew a stead-fast spirit within me.

Psalm 51:10 NKJV

THE OLD CABLE SAYING

The Bible's book of Proverbs can be an awesome blessing to one's life,
For it gives great perspective and cuts foolishness away like a knife.

And if you read only a chapter for each of the month's days,
You will gain valuable wisdom which can guide your life's ways.

For wise decisions will surely follow when we pursue our Maker's way,
And adopt the old Cable Rhyme's counsel to add steel in our steps day by day.

The earlier we know and apply "God's Good" to this wise Old Cable Rhyme,
The longer we will have to prosper and be blessed throughout our remaining lifetime.

But if poor decisions become close friends and are welcomed for many a day,
We will find the threat in the Old Cable Rhyme to capture and slowly lead us astray.

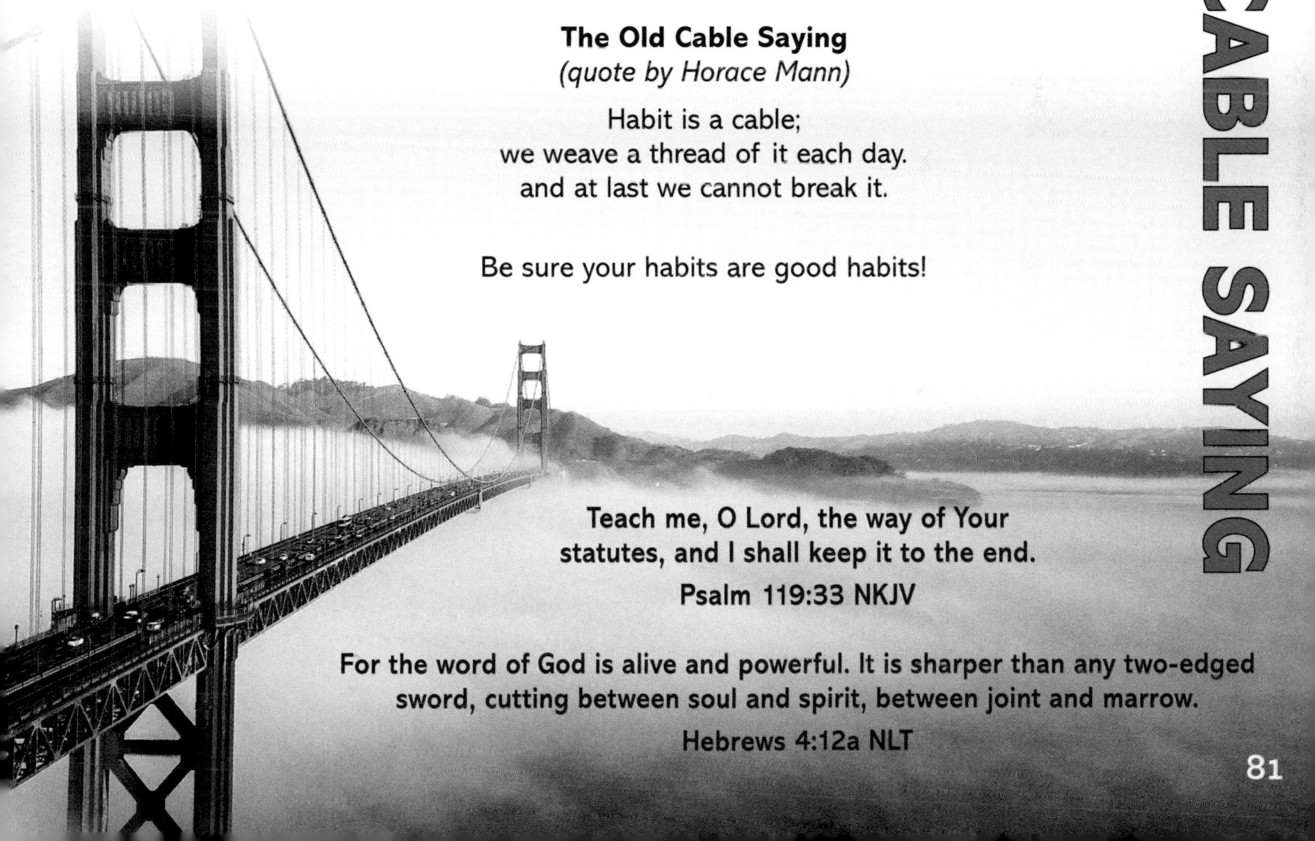

The Old Cable Saying
(quote by Horace Mann)

Habit is a cable;
we weave a thread of it each day.
and at last we cannot break it.

Be sure your habits are good habits!

Teach me, O Lord, the way of Your statutes, and I shall keep it to the end.
Psalm 119:33 NKJV

For the word of God is alive and powerful. It is sharper than any two-edged sword, cutting between soul and spirit, between joint and marrow.
Hebrews 4:12a NLT

House . . . or Home

Amazing what we devote to a house here on earth,
When time thus expended could be of far greater worth.

For time and money put into an earthly house valued high,
May devalue one's final home in the sweet by and by.

For on earth gold and opulence can soon become a bore,
When one finds there is fading hope in just adding more.

And that plush house possession once viewed as a must,
Has robbed us as we realize that we are both bound for dust.

Toil for a mansion adds nothing for heaven's bank to store,
While souls live forever when death unlocks the last door.

True, a grand house may make us proud for a short while,
But later be used and abused by the next owner's life style.

But souls can shine on forever in a new wonderful place,
If they hear of the Savior and accept God's amazing grace.

For God has promised a mansion for believing souls to claim,
Who have put trust in Jesus and understand why He came.

And the Bible speaks of peace and it is comforting to learn,
Jesus prepares a new home in heaven and will soon return.

So don't work for just a house wherever you may roam,
And, be it ever so humble, make your house a Christian home.

Gospel love can then bring neighbors and friends to our Lord,
As your home becomes a beacon light to guide them on board.

And good works in His name can be treasure sent ahead,
Where rust cannot tarnish, or mold and decay are dead.

So before locking all net worth in some luxurious dwelling,
Remember, too soon it will be just a house someone is selling.

Just don't let a costly house inhibit your kingdom-work mode,
And remember, Jesus came to change neighbors' eternal abode.

"For the Son of Man has come to save that which was lost."

Matthew 18:11 NKJV

"In My Father's house are many mansions; if *it were* not *so*, I would have told you. I go to prepare a place for you."

John 14:2 NKJV

Pride *goes* before destruction, and a haughty spirit before a fall. Better *to be* of a humble spirit with the lowly.
Proverbs 16:18 – 19a NKJV

Bicycle Lore

Today as usual I took my bike to the trail,
But there I was met by a very stiff gale.

Since the wind would be mostly upon my back,
I decided to give it a try and took to the track.

With the wind now behind me, I sailed along fast,
And gave little thought to the trip home as time quickly passed.

Then I glanced at my watch and an hour had flown by,
The ride home would be tough as the clouds rushed by.

As wind gusts made my progress seem to stand still,
I lowered my head and pretended I was going uphill.

I imagined I was younger and in a major bicycle race,
And had passed everyone and now was running in first place.

When I finally arrived back at our adult mobile park,
I was sure glad I had made it back before it turned dark.

That evening we joined a group of friends who were all in their eighties,
And my day's adventure really seemed to impress most of the ladies.

Tales of my younger bike-riding races appeared to wax great,
Till my wife's look clearly said, "Your stories are too strong. It's getting late."

And as I looked at the group's countenance as a story-teller often does,
I had to sheepishly confess, "Well, the older I get, the better I was".

God's Awesome College Gift

When a boy, life seemed to pass so slow,
But it sure picked up fast when off to IU I did go.

One day hurrying across campus and late for class,
I saw coming my way the most beautiful lass.

And as she came closer my heart skipped a beat,
Could this be the girl I prayed someday to meet?

When her flashing blue eyes glanced over at me,
She was by far the prettiest lass I ever did see.

Her lovely brown hair framed a blush and sweet smile,
Which captivated my thoughts in class the whole while.

Although as a boy, I had prayed to find the right girl,
I was surprised how this coed put my mind in a whirl.

My quest became seeing her again at all cost,
But as days passed by I feared all hope might be lost.

Till one evening in the library while studying a book,
My friend saw a girl and said, "Wow ...take a look!"

When I scooted my chair a little to the right,
Seeing her again confirmed my love at first sight.

As she leaned to her left, our eyes met once more,
But with a blush on her face, she slipped out the door.

The friends at her table protected her from my call,
For they would not reveal her name or residence hall.

But my love for Beverly Sue was destined to be,
And before very long she was there studying with me.

I never looked back or wanted to date anyone new,
For my love at first glance just grew and grew.

And when she took my pin at a Delta Chi serenade,
I knew this was the best college decision I had ever made.

Before long we were walking down the church aisle,
As her hometown friends and family all wore a happy smile.

Happy days with few tears flew by at a fast pace,
With four wonderful children adding more love to the race.

And soon grandchildren brought us still more great joy,
As we hugged five awesome girls and three terrific boys.

And we now wonder how life could have flown by so fast,
As we realize sixty years of great marriage have now passed.

And while life's journey will fade our youthful beauty some,
My sweetheart's inward beauty glows stronger and will never be done.

And someday when we share everlasting life
without care,
I will again thank God for Beverly, the perfect answer
to my prayer.

Love ... God's Greatest Gift!

Love is patient, love is kind. It does not envy, it does not boast, it is not proud. It does not dishonor others, it is not self-seeking, it is not easily angered, it keeps no record of wrongs. Love does not delight in evil but rejoices with the truth. It always protects, always trusts, always hopes, always perseveres. Love never fails.

1 Corinthians 13: 4 – 8a NIV

Me, Blue and an Old Chair Too

Is there anything as inviting as your comfortable old chair?
For it always seems to be ready for your respite there.

And when your body is tired and your strength does wane,
This old friend can lull you to sleep and have you feeling no pain.

For your old chair knows how to caress your unique shape,
And give your tired body a better lift than Superman's cape.

And try as you may to stay awake for the news,
You fall asleep and miss hearing all those pessimistic views.

For sweet dreams may lead down a fun trail for you,
As your old dog Blue snuggles in for some dream-travel too.

And you may both escape trouble and care for a while,
As God's grace frees your mind from the TV dial.

When you lie down, you will not be afraid; yes, you will lie down your sleep will be sweet.
Proverbs 3:24 NKJV

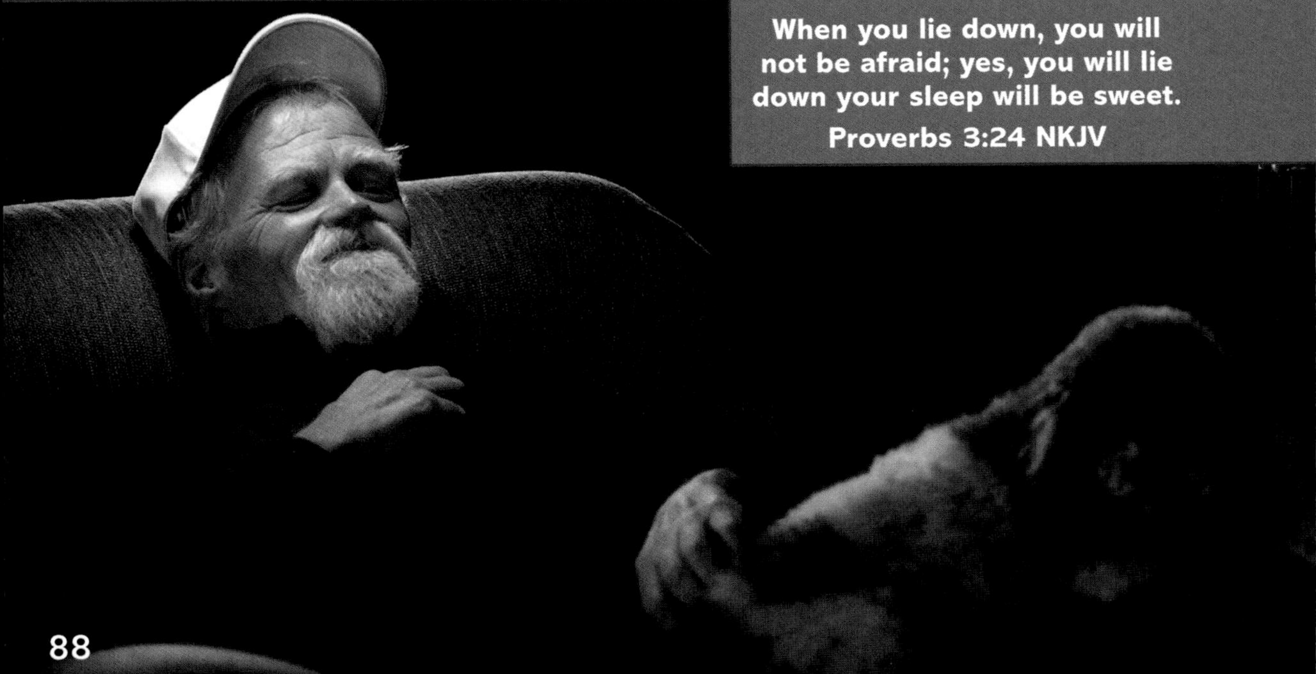

The Hourglass

When our hourglass is turned over and sand begins to flow,
It seems when a child that the sand moves so very slow.

As a teen the sand's flow seems to speed up so much,
For we have places to go and many people to touch.

Ah, but when we meet that special one, happy times fly,
And sand races through the glass like pretty clouds in the sky.

Love and marriage bring joy with kids and grandkids galore,
And as we gage our hourglass sand, we wish for much more.

When all the kids move away and our hair turns to gray,
Top sand disappears quickly as we slow down day by day.

But we both smile at God's promises as we reach for a cane,
For in His heaven, life is forever with no hourglass or pain.

And the prayer on our lips as the last grains slide through;
Is may our Family Circle join us, unbroken and all new.

"Now this is eternal life:
that they know you, the only
true God, and Jesus Christ,
whom you have sent."

John 17:3 NIV

Sensing God's
Great Love

A morning walk can be an awesome thing to enjoy!
But do I take for granted the God-given senses I employ?

My eyes view the flowers that bless my way as I go,
And my heart jumps for joy for His love they do show.

The song of a sweet bird soon embraces my ear,
Could it be saying, "God surely loves you, my dear?"

I feel a gentle breeze blow softly across my brow,
And I love the cool feeling He has sent and wonder how.

As I round the last bend He spreads delight in the air,
For I catch the sweet smell of apple pie from somewhere.

I quickly open my house door to find pastry cooling on the table,
And one bite excites my taste buds as only apple pie is able.

I thank Him and ask how could five senses provide any more?
Till love's sixth sense comes with a kiss from the wife I adore.

Again I pause to thank God for senses bestowed from above,
And thank Jesus for our everlasting relationship paid for by love.

And I wonder if in heaven my senses will still be limited to five,
Or be unlimited for the saints His love brings back alive.

And while I know in this life my five senses will soon pale,
The love relationship won by our Savior for eternity will not fail!

Give thanks to the God of heaven. ***His love endures forever.***

Psalm 136:26 NIV

Hearing His Voice in Song

Oh what blessed words reside in the great old hymns,
That thrill my soul and give a wonderful picture of Him.

For simply knowing, "Jesus paid it all, and all to Him I owe,"
Causes His sweet peace and love in my heart to flow.

And hearing, "Blessed assurance Jesus is mine,"
Gives me assurance God's love will never resign.

And singing, "How firm a foundation ... is found in His Word,"
Gives me faith in the Bible where sure guidance is heard.

And the sweet truth, "Jesus loves me, this I know,"
Fills me with joy as out into my Father's world I go.

While I can rejoice in the repetition of a praise and worship refrain,
Where the band waxes louder and louder and voices do strain.

What I love most is the sound-theology of the grand old hymns,
Where the Holy Spirit's, "Still Small Voice," touches my heart within.

For when my praise flows with no work or self-convincing from me,
My soul is captured by, "Oh how He loves you and me."

And after the fire a
still small voice.

1 Kings 19:12b NKJV

By this we know
that we abide in
Him, and He in us,
because He has
given us of His Spirit.

1 John 4:13 NKJV

Captured by a Song

How quickly a song can sweep the memories of your mind,
And bring back words long forgotten, till you remember every line.

And a longing warmth comes over you, as her presence fills the room,
Till it seems you catch a fragrance of her captivating perfume.

Soon you're gliding across the floor as you hold her very near,
As she smiles and softly whispers, "I love you so much, my dear."

Her blue eyes sparkle with the gleam of untold bliss,
And your lips begin to tingle as you anticipate her kiss.

When your precious day-dream seems so good it must be true,
The song and memory fade and she is no longer there with you.

And as you marvel how a song could so touch your very heart,
You realize some sweet song memories never really do depart.

So you share this memory trip with your bride of sixty-plus years,
And both thank God for such a happy memory when by a song it reappears.

He who finds a wife finds a good *thing*, and obtains favor from the Lord.

Proverbs 18:22 NKJV

THE GREAT PARK DISCOVERY

My habit had become to have lunch in the park,
For it lifted my spirits to be out of the dark.

Our lunch room was neat and our food was the best,
But food on a park bench gave my mind a needed rest.

I would pick up a sandwich at the Vickery Dock,
And avoid conversation with peers wanting to talk shop.

There was a bench which seemed to be reserved for just me,
With a tree to offer shade or sun, whichever was to be.

Across University Park stood the college I attended for a while,
And thoughts of those happy days often caused me to smile.

One day I was joined by a man whose countenance was magnetic,
And I recognized him as the renowned professor, Dr. Rettick.

A conversation followed which we both enjoyed very much,
So we decided to meet twice weekly for lunch and simply "go Dutch."

He was deep in academics and I became his personal student,
While I gave him insight into investments which were prudent.

Psychology, philosophy and history were interests of mine,
And Dr. Rettick waxed eloquently with wisdom each day we would dine.

I am afraid my contribution to our association was quite small,
I helped him some with investing but gained a master's degree by it all.

On good weather days, our meetings continued for many a year,
Until he announced he could no longer meet with me here.

He would be leaving to become Dean of a great western college,
And while my eyes teared up, I thanked him for sharing all the knowledge.

Then I posed my final question before he took his great wisdom away,
"What is the greatest truth you would pass along to me on this day?"

He said, "Your question is wise and I must answer before I go.
It's simply, Jesus loves me, this I know, for the Bible tells me so."

The fear of the Lord *is* the beginning of wisdom.

Proverbs 9:10a NKJV

We love Him because He first loved us.

1 John 4:19 NKJV

Cynicism

Casting all your care upon Him, for He cares for you.

1 Peter 5:7 NKJV

Today I passed a friend who called a greeting to me,
Good morning, Jim, I hope it will be so for thee.

As I took a few more steps a thought flashed through my mind,
Sam normally speaks as a critic who I never feel is kind.

A mocking bird landed singing her beautiful song,
I marveled at how the Creator could bring this blessing along.

But a noisy crow drowned out my private serenade,
And my mind asked if this is merely a charade.

As I paused by a garden with sun on the flowers,
It was sure a delight to my wandering eye.
And my eyes puddled as I marveled His gift given to a solitary soul such as I.

But then I noticed some weeds choking out part of this beauty,
And my thankful heart was conflicted with thoughts of weeding duty.

The smells from the bakery floated from my next stop,
And my thought of the tastes was a delight hard to top.

Then a thought crossed my mind if this sense was meant to bless,
For my weight is too heavy and my exercise has become less.

A new sign to my right said a church would be built there,
Was this an answer to what seemed the impossible congregational prayer?

But again my mind strayed down a silly doubt-trail,
As I wondered if Mr. Coincidence was merely reading our mail.

It is easy to be cynical about God's ways,
For satan works overtime to lead us astray.

But time spent in the Bible and petitions in prayer,
Can give our faith wings and relieve a worried world of care.

Walking with Worry

With an anxious heart I ventured out for a walk,
But a troubled mind shut my senses to God talk.

For the flowers which so often speak joy as I go,
Seemed hidden from sight by weeds from below.

And when a robin hopped gaily across my way,
I did not even hear his sweet song for the day.

Even the breeze was contrary and blew dust in my face,
And I fretted that to neighbors I would look a disgrace.

As I approach our back door there was a smell in the air,
I wondered if there was a fire in our house somewhere.

But as I threw open the back door I found no alarm,
Just peach pies cooling on the table all safe from harm.

My wife's kiss on my cheek made me turn over a new leaf,
As her love changed my perspective from negative belief.

For this morning my five senses had seen only bad,
When God gives so much for which I should be glad.

And as I confessed my heart had been focused on harm,
God refreshed my mind to His wide world full of charm.

And a voice to my soul said, "Come with Me and be joyful.
Quit seeking life's flaw which only make your mind doleful."

As I glanced at my calendar with a Bible verse for the day,
I took heart in the Proverb which will now guide my way.

But let all those rejoice who put their trust in You.

Psalm 5:11a NKJV

Cloud Play

When fluffy clouds drift by, there's a fun game to play,
For clouds form many animals which slowly fade away.

You may picture a duck, a unicorn, or even a fish,
In fact, you can find almost any creature you wish.

Girls often find kittens and little lambs and such,
But with boys, domestic animals … not so much.

Boys often see lions, tigers and bears floating by,
Which morph into the most fearsome creatures of the sky.

And while the girls enjoy pointing out animals found on the farms,
Boys point-out a Triceratops or T-Rex with big teeth and little arms.

If storm clouds with lightning are blowing in from the west,
It's then a fire-breathing Dragon can be envisioned the best.

If a Dragon's fire and thunder makes your hair stand on end,
It's game over, find a safe place, no time left to pretend!

Then He arose and rebuked the wind, and said to the sea, "Peace, be still!" And the wind ceased and there was a great calm.

Mark 4:39 NKJV

And they feared exceedingly, and said to one another, "Who can this be, that even the wind and sea obey Him!"

Mark 4:41 NKJV

Self Talk

> "For the Son of Man has come to save that which was lost."
>
> Matthew 18:11 NKJV

I found I was conversing with myself today,
And discovered I had quite a lot to say.

I had little on deposit to answer most of my queries,
So back and forth I went until I became quite weary.

Then a third party entered my vigorous debate,
And whispered, "You know My help would really be great!"

Then I remembered past blessings of the Counselor's Word,
The One with all wisdom from whom I had often heard.

A peace filled my soul when I realized He was there,
As I thought to myself, "You have again ignored prayer."

And the One with all wisdom did His promised part,
As He shut out the clutter which troubled my heart.

His gracious love made my prayers even bolder,
As He lifted the load I had placed upon my shoulders.

No longer was conversation wrapped up in self talk,
But laced with faith, hope, and love to strengthen my walk.

Then the cares of this world seemed to fade by the wayside,
And an hour flew by as I conversed with my Guide.

When I returned to the world of trouble and care,
My mind was on God's love, and His peace was now there.

The Magic Old Bench

Behold, children *are* a heritage from the Lord.
Psalm 127:3a NKJV

What a delightful pair are our grandkids, Ronnie and Renee.
And what a blessing was ours when these twins came our way.

Bev and I had prayed for grandkids for so many years,
Before we were finally blessed by these remarkable dears.

We often prayed before meals at MCL Cafeteria back then,
And sometimes on an outside old bench while awaiting a friend.

This old bench became a magic pal as time passed,
Which shared our joy when our twins came at last.

And the magic old bench whispered reminders as time flew by:
"I held the girls for the happy photos which now tear-up your eye."

The years of dolls and toys melted away like morning dew on the grass,
But the magic old bench photos could bring memories back in a flash.

Following days of school and work stole picture opportunities away,
As increased activity made it tough to find an MCL dining day.

The magic old bench continued to serve on with grace,
And looked forward to still being our very special photo place.

Again it seemed but a blink of the eye till the twins were in college,
And picture time gave way to a quest for wisdom and knowledge.

The magic old bench still hung around awaiting our twin cast,
And whispered, "I hope I can still help chronicle your grandkids' past."

Now we still occasionally all meet at MCL for a fun family event,
And I recall the days of prayer before God's twin answer was sent.

Yesterday the magic old bench bid me to glance over its way,
And whispered, "A new picture with Ronnie and Renee could sure make my day!"

Well, we thank the magic old bench for memory pictures of love,
As we share our twins' dreams, and God's will and grace from above.

The Long View

"God so loved the world, that he gave his only begotten Son, that whosoever believeth in him should not perish, but have everlasting life."
John 3:16 KJV

It was a long way down from the Grand Hotel to the lake,
But the view from the front porch was beyond just great.

As I sat down by an old man who was dressed up so fine,
He invited me to join him for a glass of his wine.

I accepted his offer as we awaited supper together,
And our conversation focused on the magnificent weather.

But as our talk moved along to his younger days,
I was fascinated by his wisdom and keen winning ways.

We conversed while the sun settled over the lake,
He was so at peace and he whispered, "God sure is great!"

When I ask how he gained such peace along the way,
He replied, "Just take the long view of life, each and every day."

Our days here on earth are really quite short,
Compared to an eternity spent on the Lord's front porch."

As we watched a sailboat skillfully guided to port,
He said, "Only God's grace can keep us truly on course.

Distractions will tempt you to detour from the right way,
But don't let them lure you off course and mess up your day.

Listen to God's Spirit and keep His long view,
You will see Jesus purchased everlasting life for me and for you.

But you must accept this free gift bestowed by God's love,
And trust the Bible promises sent down from above."

His eyes then closed as he took his last breath in that chair,
But the stranger's long view of life became real to me there.

I will remember forever the incredible gift given me that day,
For peace and joy are now mine along God's everlasting way.

What's in a Name

While one's first name may be Tom, Dick, or Harry,
It is not the name that matters, but how it is carried.

For both saints and scoundrels have worn each name,
And their words and actions are sure not the same.

So if one wants to bring honor to their given name,
It's up to them whether the result is shame or fame.

And while a nickname may add an external twist to one's goal,
It is what we put deep inside that will own and empower each soul.

For even Ichabod can be a name where joy in life is charted,
Although in Hebrew Ichabod means, "The glory has departed."

When one is born again and the Holy Spirit invades their life,
They can escape the name-identity which previously earned them strife.

And when our earthly life is over and heaven becomes our new home,
God promises an amazing new name written upon a white stone.

He who believes in the Son has everlasting life.
John 3:36a NKJV

"And I will give him a white stone, and on the stone a new name written which no one knows except him who receives it."
Revelation 2:17b NKJV

Arrogance Uncovered

Pride *goes* before destruction, and a haughty spirit before a fall.

Proverbs 16:18 NKJV

As I sat on my bed, I thought about my day,
Then I dropped to my knees and started to pray.

And I felt very good about how I had conducted my life,
For I had done some good deeds to relieve others' strife.

As I thought of those poor people captured by sin,
I was glad no temptation had made me give in.

Then my mind focused on the bad things
I could have done.
Wow! I had not even told a lie ..... well, not a
big one.

But then the Holy Spirit whispered, "Remember
your time with Jim after church.
You sure bragged a lot with no interest in his
God-search."

Then I confessed that sly sin which had caused
me to boast,
As I recalled that pride and arrogance are what
God hates the most.

If we confess our sins, He is faithful and just to forgive us *our* sins and to cleanse us from all unrighteousness.

1 John 1:9 NKJV

Dream Flights

Have you ever dreamed you could fly through the air,
Over farms and fields or the skyscrapers there?

Well this is my favorite dream in the night,
For it seems I soar effortlessly without using my might.

And no worry or care seems to hinder my way,
Though my flight may be at home or oceans away.

Since I can't plan an itinerary or where my flights will go,
I travel to many strange new places I don't even know.

And my trips are so happy when I soar up there,
That I hate to wake up to this world filled with care.

My mind is at ease and free to go any place,
So I travel fearlessly at warp speed through outer space.

When I do awaken, REM sleep has washed worry away,
And I feel rested and enthused about God's amazing new day.

Sometimes I do linger and sit wondering on my bed,
How will we travel in heaven when our earthly bodies are dead?

And if we have accepted the new birth from Jesus in our bodies here,
How will our new heavenly body perform and appear?

Jesus answered and said to him, "Most assuredly, I say to you, unless one is born again, he cannot see the kingdom of God."

John 3:3 NKJV

For this perishable must clothe itself with the imperishable, and the mortal with immortality.

1 Corinthians 15:53 NIV

None to Son

Today I met a man on a walk with his young son,
We talked of Jesus who he proclaimed was God's son.

He said, "Jesus is the answer to what life is all about,
And He is the answer to coping with one's doubt."

He told how Christian faith had freed him from strife,
For Christ said, "I am the way, the truth, and the life."

To his appeal, I replied, "Well, I would rather be a "none",
For people *without* religion just seem to have more fun.

And for me, my faith shall revolve around just one,
I will trust in myself till my life on earth is done.

Prayer to me is a crutch for those who are weak,
And I won't bow down with those who are meek.

I don't care whether man's beginning just came from slime,
To me all that intellectual speculation ain't worth a dime.

And why I am here now and where I will go,
Shall not trouble me, for I'm just a free so-and-so.

I plan to do as I please and do things my own way,
And I don't really care what the Bible may say.

Who needs the Bible to act as their guide,
For my pursuit is happiness which I hope lies inside."

My new friend's son turned with a tear in his eye,
And I felt bad when I realized he was about to cry.

Then I noticed that tucked under his arm was The Book,
And Bible memories of promises to my soul became a hook.

For as a youth I had heard of a Savior who loved me so,
But doubt had robbed me and I had let my faith go.

Now I thought of a personal God who loved me,
And it brought tears as God's Spirit made my way hard to see.

But when I walked by a church on the way I must go,
The voices of a children's choir rang out soft and low.

The sweet refrain of, "Jesus loves me, this I know,"
Was followed by assurance, "For the Bible tells me so."

Again I noticed my acquaintance without his young son,
And I apologized for any harm my comments had done.

He noticed the great change of attitude on my part,
For the Spirit had removed the doubt-lock on my heart.

We talked about heaven, the Bible, and so much more,
Until the music ended and his son opened the church door.

The boy ran to his father ... as I was now running to mine,
And by my smiling face he knew it was a very good sign.

The son held out his Bible and said, "Please accept this from me,"
And his father's nod let me know he would like this to be.

My eyes puddled again as I finished my course,
For I felt joy and relief from past memories and remorse.

When home I let the Bible fall open for a surprise,
For John 3:16 did glisten through tears in my eyes.

And Belief said, "You are no longer a "none,"
And Faith said, "Welcome home, my lost son!"

"And how shall they believe in Him of whom they have not heard?"

Romans 10:14b NKJV

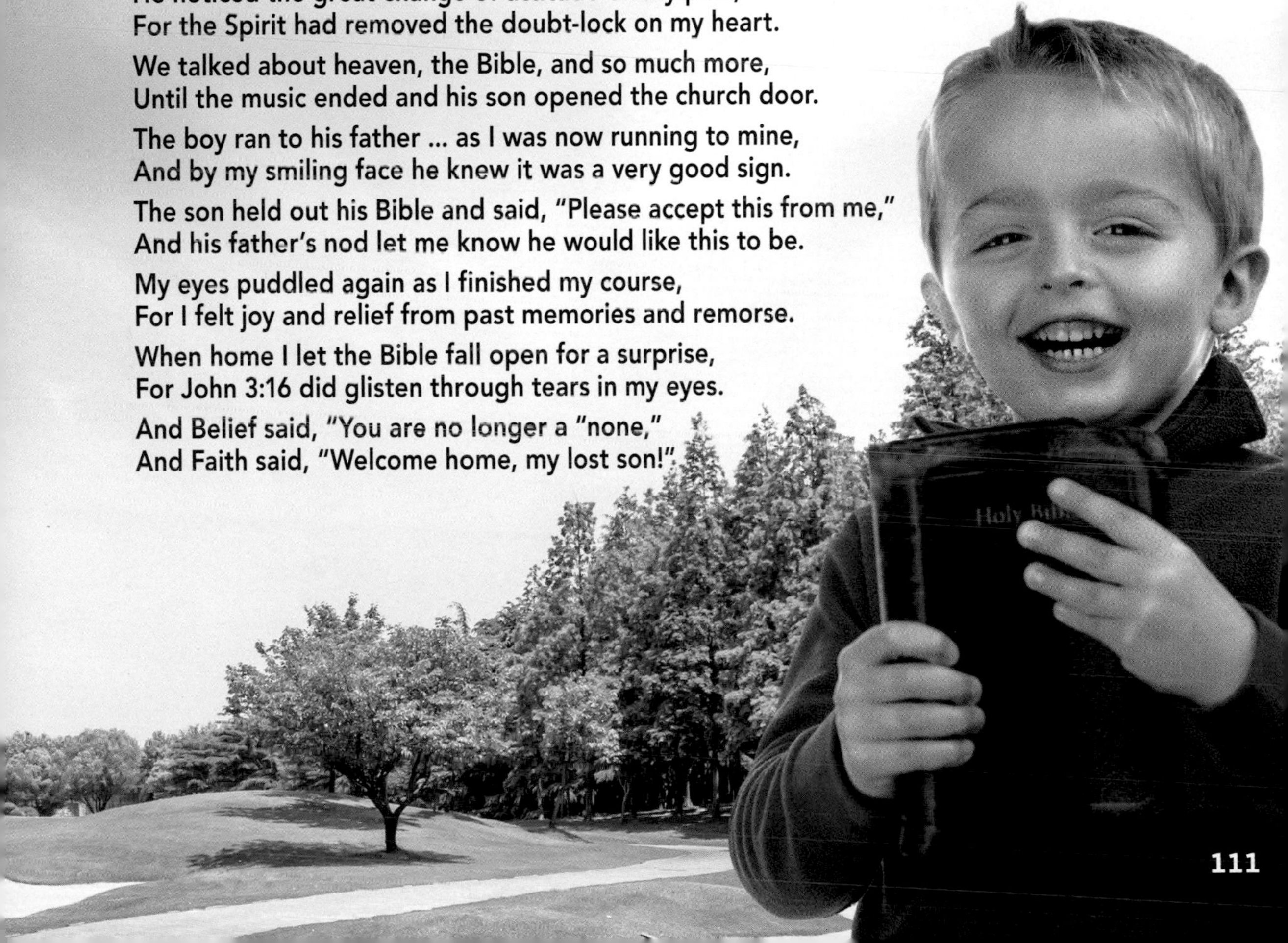

Soul Searching

It seems nothing in God's universe completely goes away,
It just takes on a new form that is still somewhere today.

It may turn to water, gas, other matter, or just clay,
So should a Soul not also be eternal and here to stay?

Theories on how we were made from nothing do abound,
But our mind and very being confirm our Soul is around.

And while the physical Soul in our body can't by a medical scan be seen,
Still it encompasses our intellect, emotion, and will ... and gives power
to our being.

"For what will it profit a man if he gains the whole world, and loses his own soul?"

Mark 8:36 NKJV

"For God so loved the world that He gave His only begotten Son, that whoever believes in Him should not perish but have everlasting life."

John 3:16 NKJV

Our personality and talents confirm each Soul to be one of a kind,
And common sense says a Master Creator must have given humans their incredible mind.

Macro-Space exploration provides no physical Soul source origination clue at all,
And when we delve into Nano-space, there seems no end to what we find to call small.

So our whole life records may exist on a Soul-chip smaller than an atom,
Where there's no hope for others to probe and set their eyes on them.

But would God destroy a Soul masterpiece which He loves and made to enjoy,
To whom He has endowed god-like power on earth to will, do and employ?

True, sin entered our world and put hope and life limitations on each Soul,
But also true is the invisible New Birth which can cleanse and make a Soul whole.

While no surgeon can find the Soul to remove the sin with a knife,
We see that being born again by faith can make an amazing change in one's life.

So why should "Born Again" be so hard to accept as true,
When no scientist can even explain the Soul and why there is a 'you'?

But there is one true record of history and wisdom from the past,
Which explains the Soul's genesis and a future which forever will last.

For the Holy Bible is an owner's manual for all who accept John 3:16 as true,
With words of love, wisdom, guidance, and eternal hope to the Soul that is you.

John 14:6 tells of "the way, the truth, and the life" who came to rescue our Soul,
For Jesus is God's Son, who suffered, bled and died in your place accomplishing this goal.

Since we can't scan our Soul physically while our body does live,
We must take it by faith that our unseen Soul contains a life after death to give.

The Bible promises the born-again Soul will experience
God's amazing grace,
In a new heavenly body and not merely floating somewhere in space.

So when a Soul receives salvation by grace through faith in Jesus Christ alone,
The Holy Spirit will guide their invisible Soul to a wonderful new everlasting home.

The Chime's Magic Helpers

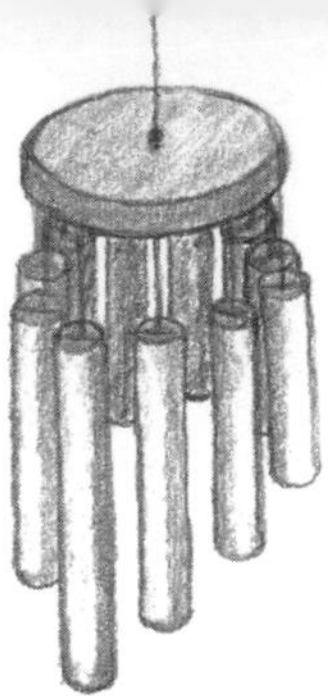

What sweet sounds one hears when
chimes are gently kissed by a breeze,

For they sing soft chords that put
a child's active mind at ease.

For the steel rings-out new
tunes, never before known,

And some say little Pixies direct
this music, all on their own.

But at night if you pull up the covers,
and peak out of one eye,

You may see shy Pixies chime-swinging,
and one may even fly by.

But you must resist the strong power
of their enchanting chime tune,

For it spreads magic vibrations which
will lure you to Dreamsville, too soon.

A fairy tale poem by James R. Anthony & art by Byron T.

CAPTURED BY THE SEA

> The earth *is* the Lord's, and all its fullness, the world and those who dwell therein. For He has founded it upon the seas, and established it upon the waters.
>
> Psalm 24:1-2 NKJV

How neat to hear the rhythm of waves rolling in,
As the wind and the tide seem to be fully akin.

Your sunglasses catch a sparkle on each wave curl,
To delight your eyes like the smile of a happy school girl.

And the fragrance of sun lotion and sea-spray tease your brain,
Like the tiny bubbles from a glass of sparkling champagne.

And even the sea-salt as it is forming on your lips,
Brings a taste-sensation you don't want to miss.

So you settle back on the sand to enjoy a soft breeze on your skin,
And thank God for giving you five senses to take this all in.

As you fight sleep and try to catch jumping dolphins at play,
You dose-off and dreams of shy mermaids whisk you away.

Birth of a Buisness

It all starts with a vision born in the recesses of your mind,
Which is driven by a passion to see this intriguing idea refined.

Common sense says, "Wake-up!" this innovation can never become real,
But the vision lingers as hope whispers, "This could be the real deal."

And soon you are captured by Mr. Possibility and Mrs. Pursuit,
So you cast the word *can't* aside and search for other dreamers to recruit.

You borrow money to supplement your savings and give you a start,
While confidants remind you a fool and his money will soon part.

Now you do see how Mr. Opportunity and Brother Risk walk hand in hand,
Which improves your prayer life and the pursuit of wisdom to understand.

Remember, before diving into the water to ask, "Could God truly bless and own such a venture as mine?"
And if by God's grace this seems to be so, write a Christian Mission and Core Values to keep your heart in line.

Then to keep this new creation from becoming your master,
Commit its ownership to God to avoid pride and personal disaster.

Business success can seem sweet until it steals a part of your soul,
But when Jesus owns it all, you can be at peace and remain whole.

And should God's Providence permit this venture to fail,
You will suffer no personal loss and your soul's health can prevail.

And whatever you do, do it heartily, as to the Lord and not to men.

Colossians 3:23 NKJV

The Old Fisherman's Rhyme

"When the wind is from the East the fishes bite the least.
When the wind is from the North the fishes don't come forth.
When the wind is from the West the fishes bite the best.
But when the wind is from the South, it blows the bait in the fishes' mouth."

I have often talked with fishermen about this Old Rhyme and they generally
agree it rings true, most of the time.

One day the south wind coaxed the girls to go fish with us guys,
And while not much into fishing, they loved the soft breeze and clear skies.

But soon the fish the girls were catching, kept us busy baiting their line.
Which was fun for us guys and meant the meals ahead would sure be fine.

After catching our walleye limit, we put tiny lures on each girl's pole,
And then settled back to just relax, with our boat on a slow fish troll.

But that's when the South wind decided to live up to her fame,
For blowing the girl's bait into the mouths of big fish became her aim.

And soon our iPhones were taking pictures of the south wind's winning game,
To document the girl's huge trophy walleye and northern pike claim.

Now I see what a kind South wind can really do,
To make an Old Fisherman's Rhyme a believer of you.

But we really praise God who made us, the fish, the wind, and it all,
And thank Him for granting the south wind her amazing and effective
fish call.

*Then God said, "Let us make mankind
in our image, in our likeness, so that
they may rule over the fish in the sea"
Genesis 1:26a NIV*

To See by the Sea

I walked along the high cliffs by the sea today,
And the view I took in was incredible to say.

As the breakers crashed upon the high rock wall,
My steps took care to avoid a last fall.

In youth I skipped this path without care,
But now as a senior my mind bids beware.

I enjoy the same view though my eyes are now dim,
But know I must stay even closer to Him.

For evil still temps me to stray from God's care,
And step off the path He graciously put there.

But when I glance back to my stumbling stride,
I see my Savior was there to guide by my side.

And now I proceed relieved of all fear,
Knowing to my journey's end, He will always be near.

To guide my steps should my mind's eye fade,
From that sure destination His loving hands have made.

And while the sea in the sunset is awesome to see,
It will be nothing to what He has waiting for me.

In My Father's house are many mansions.
John 14:2a NKJV

Sands of Time

The sands of time move so slowly during our first days,
That when a child at play, time seems hard to fritter away.

But as the hourglass sands in the bottom collect,
School days rush by as we grow tall and erect.

And when courtship and marriage enter the scene,
Days fly by so swiftly the sand's change is not seen.

The joy of kids brings to your home much laughter,
But when young ones are gone you see the sand has moved faster.

And as you settle down to quieter days with only your wife,
The bottom sand sneaks on higher as grandkids brighten your life.

But before you can grasp it, you are now turning the last page,
And a glance at the sand confirms you have reached old age!

And as the sand in the bottom begins to settle at rest,
You take hope in Christ's promise of an eternity blest!

For God so loved the world that He gave His only begotten Son, that whoever believes in Him should not perish but have everlasting life.

John 3:16 NKJV

Snow Dreaming

While shoveling the snow off our walk and driveway,
My mind drifted through falling flakes to a much earlier day.

As a kid after chores, I pondered what to do and where to go,
Unless Old Man Winter began laying down a white blanket of snow.

For then clear direction exploded out of the white glow,
As kids came running for Monster Hill by Battle Plateau.

And it seems I can almost hear the cry of Wild Sledder Joe,
When he slid blindfolded down the hill yelling, "Beware below!"

And I can almost see pretty little Jill on the back of big brother Jack,
For she was always smiling over my way as I happily smiled back.

Back then looking down Monster Hill rivaled a view down from the Alps to below,
But now this height vision has sure shrunk as I reminisce to back fifty years ago.

A parking lot has gobbled up where terrific snow battles once took place,
And black asphalt, curbs, and signs have desecrated our magical space.

For in by-gone day snow forts and mighty warriors possessed these lands,
But now fancy vehicles and shoppers have replaced our battling bands.

And Old Screaming Mountain and Battle Plateau have become just another big fancy mall,
Which have no intrigue and sense of adventure to give mighty snow warriors a call.

I still thrill when Old Man Winter starts to lay down a carpet of snow,
And happy childhood memories and visions are still delivered in the soft white glow.

But now a far greater joy comes over me when snow begins to fall,
For I see God's love and majesty and drink in His blessed control over all.

"He sends out His command *to the* earth; His word runs very swiftly. He gives snow like wool."

Psalm 147:15-16 NKJV

The Rocking Chair's Passion

My chore for Saturday was causing delay,
For cleaning the attic didn't qualify as play.

And as I moved old stuff no longer needed around,
I came upon something big, under a blanket and bound.

Curiosity brought a tinge of excitement to my chore,
As I tried to remember what was in this long-ago store.

Was it imagination playing a trick on my mind?
For I heard a voice say, "Please uncover your find!"

I quickly untied the sash and threw off the cover,
To discover below a stately rocking chair, like no other.

Its appearance for a moment seemed to give me alarm,
For a lion's faces with an open mouth was carved on each arm.

But again the whisper said, "Sit in me and rest,
And reflect on bygone days which seem to you best."

Before long, I was asleep or captured in a trance,
In a chair formed by a master as he carved each branch.

It arrived from the North Woods when Mom married Dad,
And had served family generations through days happy and sad.

A vision came of grandmother rocking in her last days,
I only knew her from photos taken before she passed away.

It seemed I heard a faint lullaby sung sweetly by Mom,
As the chair rocked us both softly and all was so calm.

But then my sister's presence moved Mom to the middle,
And Grimm's Fairy Tales were being read which scared us a little.

The Lord is my light and my salvation—whom shall I fear? The Lord is the stronghold of my life—of whom shall I be afraid?

Psalm 27:1 NIV

I felt the lion's teeth on the chair's arm close on my hand,
As we met giants and trolls and wandered strange lands.

Then the boy was alone and the chair rocked so wild,
That it tipped over backwards and threw out the child.

I heard the thump of Dad's steps and knew all was not well,
But by a knock and ring at our door, I was "saved by the bell."

Now awake I pondered how I could have dozed off this way,
But again the whisper, "Please let me serve you these days.

For you've remembered your sister and your boyhood at last,
As I took you back to your roots with fond memories of the past.

Please free me from this old attic so my service is not done,
For I can deliver true craftsmanship, a sense of history, and fun.

For long after IKEA and Cracker Barrel's chairs remain strong,
I will whisper history and safety and rock your prodigy along.

And when you meet some of your ancestors now up above,
You will find they also granted my request with much love."

As I struggled to carry my treasure down the stair,
I pondered how to tell my wife of this happening I must share.

And what could I remove from our living room décor,
To fit this unusual old friend, which I now valued more?

Then the chair whispered to me for the last time,

"Just tell the true story, all wrapped up in a rhyme."

A fairy tale conversation about an heirloom family chair.

Bicycling Through Time

With the wind in my face I bicycle along,
While memories return to when young legs were so strong.

It's not that I lack enough strength for the task,
But at age eighty-three, I now often get passed.

And boyhood days on bikes with old friends,
Return to my mind as I go around many bends.

In grade school, my bike was key to fun times,
And for a mere ten-dollar cost my dad gave birth to bike rhymes.

Today my bike costs a hundred times that amount,
With skinny tires, fancy shifting, and twenty gears to count.

A fancy red helmet sits snugly on my head,
Protection more needed back when Mom pictured me dead.

For hands which fired my BB gun while staying on pace,
Now carefully steer to remain a living part of the human race.

Today fancy shoes and bike clothes aid my travel,

With no peddle-slip soles or pant-legs which unravel.

I pass riders on bicycles wearing all types of fancy backpacks,

Some bent down over handlebars, and some flat on their backs.

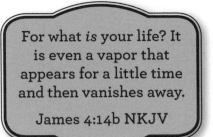

> For what *is* your life? It is even a vapor that appears for a little time and then vanishes away.
>
> James 4:14b NKJV

Some old-timers are happy to ride in the old three-wheeled ways,

The same as we all did back in our earliest tricycle days.

And as I thank God for strong legs to still make peddles go 'round,

I rejoice for the many blessings it takes for my energy to abound.

For the sights I see and the sweet sounds I hear,

Blend together with smells for invigoration so dear.

And as I marvel at all He has created for me to take in,

Happy memories float back to biking with friends and with kin.

Sometimes I envision teammates in IU's Little 500 Race,

And realize many have gone home to a much better place.

For I feel sure in heaven where many bikers now abide,

There will be awesome ways for their happy souls to ride.

But here on earth my father's early counsel rings true for me yet,

"Son, how to cycle or swim you will never forget."

A Message from my Ancestors

I took a quiet walk through the cemetary today,
In hopes of finding where my ancestor's bodies might lay.

Their life spans were etched and easy to see,
I quickly took note, that this soon would be me.

I tried to piece together family relationships which remained unclear,
And tie them together with all the history from so many years.

I had heard the stories of relatives who were remarkable women and men,
And wished I had known them all personally, and not only by paper and pen.

I knew my talents and appearance had been passed to me through their genes,
And I thought how neat to thank each one, whether poor or a person of means.

Some burial plots were marked with small and weathered stones,
While others held great monuments covering all their family's bones.

But sadly helpful epitaphs were few and far between,
Till two of them brought joy to my heart and were the most encouraging I could have seen.

For one read, "Meet me in heaven", while the other said "Not here, Gone home",
And now I know someday we will meet in the same eternal home.

"Let not your heart be troubled; you believe in God, believe also in Me. In My Father's house are many mansions; if *it were* not *so,* I would have told you. I go to prepare a place for you."

John 14:1-2 NKJV

North Woods' Pancakes

Is there any treat which greets one better than Papaw's pancakes in the morning?
For they shoo bad dreams and cares away without any warning.

When you smell those flapjacks cooking upon a steaming griddle,
Your taste buds yell, "Arise, get to the table, and don't you fiddle."

And as your ear picks up the sizzle of this culinary delight,
Your mouth begins to water as you anticipate your first bite.

When the steaming stack is finally passed along your way,
You yell, "Hey, don't keep the butter and syrup down there all day."

Right when your mouth is opened, anticipating the first delicious bite,
Mamaw's voice reminds, "Wait, we must thank the Lord for this awesome delight!"

"He gives food to every living thing.
His faithful love endures forever.
Give thanks to the God of heaven.
His faithful love endures forever."
Psalm 136: 25-26 NLT

The Wee Little Chair's Hope

Funny how a simple little old chair can become very valuable to you,
For while its street value is nil, its place in your heart remains true.

Such is the story of the wee chair which rests by the fireplace in our living room,
It was carved out over 150 years ago from the wooden handle of a pioneer's broom.

Now it ain't much to look at, but it is still sturdy and stout,
For it survived my childhood, my father and grandfather when they were
toddling about.

And now I ponder who to pass this chair of questionable value to,
For I heard it whisper by the fire, "I hope again to seat a little tot who is related
to you."

But Jesus said, "Let the little children come to Me, and do not forbid them; for of such is the kingdom of heaven."

Matthew 19:14 NKJV

Ode to Odin

I love my dog Odin and this poem is about him,
For his faith in me and my faith in my Lord indeed are akin.

For as Odin sees me as the master he loves and wishes to serve more,
I wish to serve my Master the Almighty God whom I truly adore.

As the rainbow tells of the Master's great faithfulness to mankind,
It inspires me to be master of Odin, God's golden retriever which is now mine.

Folklore tells us there is a pot of gold at the end of each rainbow,
But I wouldn't exchange golden Odin for the treasure, if that fable were so.

You will seek me and find me when
you seek me with all your heart.

Jeremiah 29:13 NIV

I have placed my rainbow in the
clouds. It is the sign of my covenant
with you and with all the earth.

Genesis 9:13 NLT

The Awesome Campus Walk

Music can take your memories back to many years ago,
And my thoughts today are of the coed who has blessed my life so.

When a teen, *true love* was a scary quest and not for me,
But I did pray as a young boy that someday a true love I would see.

I guarded my words carefully so not to portray a false view,
And when with a young lady, was careful to never say, "I love you."

But one day while in college and walking quickly to class,
My heart skipped a beat as I passed the most beautiful lass.

I glanced back to see her charms which attracted me so,
And she blushed, as her pretty blue eyes did show.

My heart gave no rest till I found this freshman once more,
And her captivating smile met me next at the library door.

For two semesters our dates always seemed much too short,
But she soon wore my pin and was the only girl I did court.

And the, I love you, which I had avoided for many a year,
Now flowed freely from my lips whenever Beverly was near.

Our magical college time flew by so fast I could cry,
And gone were college days with my "Sweetheart of Delta Chi."

Marriage followed soon after we left IU that last day,
And love's clock spun even faster to bring great blessings our way.

Four great children and eight grandkids now bless our happy estate,
As we marvel how time slipped by at such an incredible rate.

And these days I smile when I hear music's sweet, I love you, refrains,
For after our 60 married years an even stronger love remains.

And as we both look forward to sharing our love with God up above,
I thank Him for Beverly, the perfect answer to my boyhood prayer for true love.

Delight yourself also in the Lord, and He shall give you the desires of your heart.
Psalm 37:4 NKJV

Unbroken Family Circle

May Our Circle Be Unbroken in-Christ

My little son popped in just the other day and said, “Dad, please teach me to pray.” I said, “Son, not now, see what Mom has to say.”

And the days flew by as our family grew, and I was busy with so much to do.

My teen popped in with challenging questions, “Dad, why are we here and what is life all about?” I said, “Son, ask Mom. I’m on a fast track today.” And I watched as my big boy shuffled slowly away.

And the days flew by as my business boomed, and the clock’s hands spun faster as my time was consumed.

My college grad with arms round my neck said, “I love you, Dad, but who put us here and where are we headed?” I said, “Discuss that with Mom. She can explain it all.” And I watched a fine son as he walked down the hall.

And the days flew on at an incredible pace, and two handsome grandsons echoed a familiar refrain, “Papaw, please teach us to pray.” I said, “Boys, ask Mamma. She knows what to say”. And I watched as they happily scurried away.

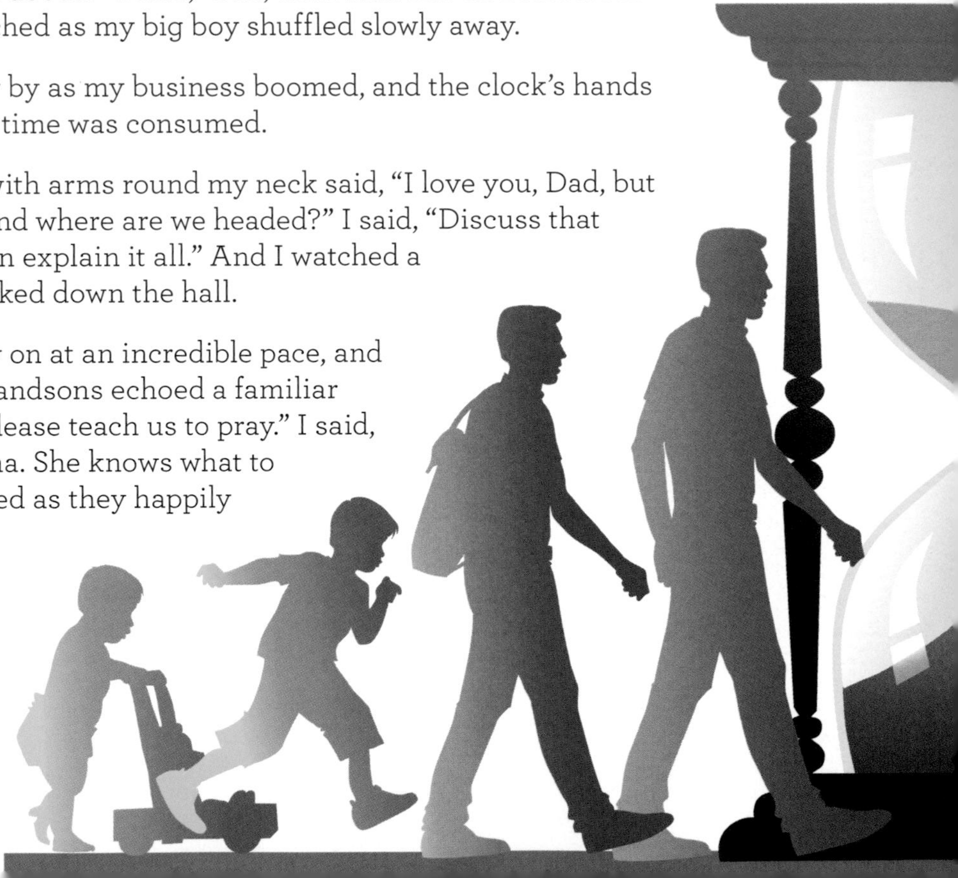

And the day's fast departure puzzled my head as I found myself surrounded and lying in bed. What my family whispers my lips are anxious to pray, "May our Family Circle with Jesus be unbroken today?"

> And Jesus said to him,
> "Assuredly, I say to you, today
> you will be with Me in Paradise."
> Luke 23:43 NKJV

And the Jesus I've neglected for so many a year like the thief on the cross, I find as my Savior here. I pray for those kids I was too busy to guide. And thank God for the Mom who prayed by their side.

As happy faces of family in tears fade from sight, my soul's securely anchored as all becomes light.

The Stone's Witness

If you were standing before the mason who'd cut the words on your tombstone today,
What would you like the size and epitaph to convey?

Would it show your wealth and achievement, or would it direct attention away from you,
And point their eyes toward the promise of Jesus that believers can be born anew?

What do you hope the mind's eye of family members and visitors will see?
Will it bring a bright hope of what meeting you in heaven someday would be?

May some visitors sense a God-shaped vacuum existing in their soul,
And seek to find our Savior Jesus and be heaven-bound and whole?

For most people would like their Soul redeemed to live on in a heavenly place,
Where perhaps there they may know friends and loved-ones even better than face-to-face.

So please request that the mason may etch upon my stone:
By God's Saving Grace through Jesus (John 3:16)

NOT HERE / GONE HOME

And though my lips now be silent and my body seem so all alone,
May some visitors grasp the soul's path to heaven from words etched upon my stone!

"For God so loved
the world that
He gave His only
begotten Son, that
whoever believes
in Him should not
perish but have
everlasting life."

John 3:16 NKJV

"Believe on the
Lord Jesus Christ,
and you will
be saved."

Acts 16:31a NKJV

Blessed Assurance Passed On

Therefore I exhort first of all that supplications, prayers, intercessions, *and* giving of thanks be made for all men.

1 Timothy 2:1a NKJV

When I was young, I was strong and could win the foot race;
But old age has taken over and slowed down my fast pace.

I now see better what is worth speeding up for,
And as my physical strength fades, I see a new prayer opportunity door.

For while strength, skill, and quick-action were once God's gifts in spades,
I now lean more wholly on prayer and Jesus' care to pervade.

Now I perceive in bygone days I gave too much credit to hard work,
And now grasp how I was just the beneficiary of God's merciful handiwork.

In troubled times and sickness God pulled me on through,
And by faith, hope, and His love, I know Christ is "the universal glue."

As I look back and thank those who prayed for my soul's survival,
I now find more time to pray for others in need of our Lord Jesus and revival.

In this manner, therefore, pray:

Our Father in heaven,
Hallowed be Your name.
Your kingdom come.
Your will be done
On earth as *it is* in heaven.
Give us this day our daily bread.
And forgive us our debts,
As we forgive our debtors.
And do not lead us into temptation,
But deliver us from the evil one.
For Yours is the kingdom and the power and the glory forever. Amen.

Matthew 6:9-13 NKJV

Ann's Song

I had a mission today which I hesitated to do,
Especially with my long-held atheistic life-view.

But soon I stood by Ann's bed with nothing to say,
As she gazed at the ceiling in a most peaceful way.

It seemed I was interrupting a very private meeting,
For she whispered so softly, but I still heard her greeting.

"It's so beautiful over there with happy people all around.
Have you seen Him! Is He anywhere to be found?"

"Oh, now I see, for His glory is everywhere.
How wonderful to be free from all earthly care."

As I started to speak she spoke my deceased brother's name,
Then she was gone. I felt I had failed and was sorry that I came.

With tears in my eyes I noticed a book on her bed,
With a note tucked-in at a highlighted section she wanted read.

It was a Bible with "Merry Christmas from Uncle Bill" on the first page,
And it fell open to where Ann's note and John 3:16 did engage.

For she wrote, "I'm so sorry I didn't say goodbye before leaving.
Please meet us in heaven and try not to be grieving."

I knelt and prayed for forgiveness for resisting God's love for so long,
And blessed Ann for highlighting Christ's peace and redemption from
all wrong.

I now pray for grace and strong faith to point others to Him!
So like Ann, my Savior's love and glory shall become my life's hymn.

“For God so loved the world
that He gave his only begotten
Son, that whoever believes
in Him should not perish but
have everlasting life.”
John 3:16 NKJV

A Sailor's Dream Fulfilled

Tommy sat alone on the dock of the bay,
Watching all the fine ships sail away.

When he told his mother, Mary, he must have a ship someday,
She smilingly replied, "Son, you better put some money away."

Tommy looked for a place to store his money,
So Mary bought a ship-bank which they agreed was funny.

And Tommy called his bank 'Piggy-Ship' and began putting in his cash,
Each time the ship-bank was filled, Mary invested his stash.

In Tommy's teen years odd jobs provided funds for his craft,
For his dream stayed alive and the bank never had to issue a draft.

When Tommy joined the Navy 'round the world he did roam,
But his mom, Mary, fed 'Piggy-Ship' any money that he sent home.

Tommy then met a Navy Wave, Sally, who shared his sailing dreams from the start,
And soon 'Piggy-Ship' funded a gold band for the love of Tommy's heart.

'Piggy-Ship' then passed from mother Mary to Tommy's wife,
For Sally and Tommy shared a love for ships as they voyaged together through life.

Tommy and Sally were blessed with Jimmy, a dear little boy of their own,
While secretly through high cost years, Sally fed 'Piggy-Ship' unbeknown.

Jimmy's college years seemed sure to torpedo the 'Piggy-Ship' dream,
But somehow side jobs and windfalls enhanced Sally's secret scheme.

And it seemed too soon for Jimmy to be married with a boy of his own,
But now grandson Bobby and Mamaw watched the ships with sails wind-blown.

And as Tommy's work days till retirement grew very short,
He noticed Mary checking out cruise pamphlets sailing to far away resorts.

By God's grace, Mary's secret investments turned out to be very wise,
And the return on her 'Piggy-Ship's' deposits steadily did maximize.

Tommy's last day at work was the day before Valentine's Day,
And that's when Mary presented him with a box marked "Piggy-Ship Pay."

And the contents sparked a dream which he had met long ago,
For he found 'Piggy Ship' and cruise tickets with so many places to go.

While Tommy had long forgotten the dream of a ship all his own,
He and Mary now had captains and a crew for sailing to every world zone.

Years of travel turned their hair to gray and put wrinkles on their faces,
But Tommy and Mary still kept 'Piggy-Ship' in the most prominent places.

And now their grandson Bobby placed coins and money in 'Piggy-Ship' for fun,
But all the family realized Tommy's life voyage would soon be done.

And as they crowded around the bed where he lay,
Tommy smiled but struggled to speak what he wanted to say.

So he pointed to a box that Mary had wrapped so nice,
And indicated it must go to his Grandson along with important advice.

And as Bobby opened the box, he found 'Piggy-Ship' enclosed,
With a note telling a story of how God's grace to him did unfold.

For he had sailed 'round the world with Mary, the girl of his dream,
With the greatest of fare and yet with no high ship expenses to glean.

And Tommy's last thoughts were etched by that smile on his face,
As he whispered, "Soon my soul must sail off to that heavenly place."

"But may my 'Piggy-Ship' prayer remind you to follow only Christ's way,
So all our family circle may be unbroken in heaven someday."

And as Tommy closed his eyes and the smile faded from his face,
His blessed soul sailed off to his Savior, by God's amazing grace.

As the family's eyes were filled with a sad but happy tear,
The attending Navy Chaplain slipped quietly out the door located in the rear.

Then they all heard him exclaim as he left with a deep sigh,
"I look forward to seeing that family's reunion in the sweet by-and-by."

Delight yourself also in the Lord, and He shall give you the desires of your heart.

Psalm 37:4 NKJV

Who can find a virtuous wife? For her worth *is* far above rubies.

Proverbs 31:10 NKJV

Smile Power

It is neat how a kind smile can lift your spirits for a while,
And shoo away the blues and adjust one's mood-dial.

For goodwill expended by this happy facial expression,
Can often bless and lift a troubled heart from depression.

My friend Charlie understood a smile's ability to ring the bell,
So when returning a smile, he added a cheerful comment as well.

For he called out, "Thank you for your smile!" and with a nod of his head
returned the smile-favor,
As he left them with a kind comment and appreciation to savor.

Now songs, and poems have long recognized a smile's power,
But try adding "Thank You" to make your return-smile an encouraging flower.

This *is* the day the Lord has made; We will rejoice and be glad in it.
Psalm 118:24 NKJV

A merry heart makes a cheerful countenance,
But by sorrow of the heart the spirit is broken.
Proverbs 15:13 NKJV

Citations

This book of poetry contains quotations, photographs and art from various sources, and multiple quotations from several versions of the *Holy Bible*. Pronouns referring to God the Father, Son, or Holy Spirit are capitalized to maintain consistent style throughout the book.

Quotes from the Holy Bible that are in quotation marks are the Word of God.

Cover image, front and back, introduction Pg. i and ii, by MJ_Prototype © iStock.com.

Introduction, To and From, Pg. i, (illustration), cutelittlethings © iStock.com.

When All Nature Sings: Pg. 1, James Richard Anthony, White Pines (photograph), courtesy James Richard Anthony.

The Mansion's Message: Pg. 2-3, (photograph), darkbird77 © iStock.com.

God's Spectacular Light Show: Pg. 4-5, (photograph), Jakob Flygare © iStock.com.

Delayed Beauty: Pg. 6, (photograph), francisLM © iStock.com.

Wild Walleye Pike: Pg. 7, (photograph), herreid © iStock.com.

Kayak Fellowship: Pg. 8-9, (photograph), wanderluster © iStock.com.

Refreshing Perspective: Pg. 10-11, (photograph), agustavop © iStock.com.

Lighting a Candle: Pg. 12, (photograph), CarlosDavid.org © iStock.com.

Through the Eyes of a Child: Pg. 14-15, (photograph), FamVeld © iStock.com.

Hidden in a String: Pg. 17, (photograph), artisteer © iStock.com.

A Tribute to Shadow: Pg. 18, (photograph), fotojagodka © iStock.com.

A Sheep's Prayer: Pg. 19, (photograph), HAYKIRDI © iStock.com.

The History Teacher's Dream: Pg. 20-21, (photograph), klikk © iStock.com.

Moving On...Without Strife: Pg. 22-23, (photograph), Gearstd © iStock.com.

A Light for Your Path: Pg. 24, (photograph), pamela_d_mcadams © iStock.com.

The Unmatched Power of God's Word: Pg. 26-27, (photograph), Vasyl Dolmatov © iStock.com.

Playing the Fool: Pg. 28, (art), koya79 © iStock.com.

Pride's Deception: Pg. 29, (photograph), chriss_ns © iStock.com.

The Mirror's Guile: Pg. 30-31, (photograph), iiievgeniy © iStock.com.

Text-Mate Awareness: Pg. 32, (photograph), Deagreez © iStock.com, Pg. 33, (illustration), ulimi © iStock.com.

Grasping the Important: Pg. 34-35, (photograph), Poike © iStock.com.

Old-Timer's Rhyme: Pg. 36-37, (photograph), scyther5 © iStock.com, Pg. 37, (illustration), ulimi © iStock.com.

The Power of Kind Words: Pg. 38, photograph, SDI Productions, © iStock.com.

Remembering My Day-Maker: Pg. 39, (photograph), AlinaMD © iStock.com.

The Fish's Sermon: Pg. 40, Twilight Muskie© (art), Terry Doughty, artist. Terry is a nationally know wildlife artist, and has won over thirty major awards since 1988. All rights reserved, image courtesy of Christine Doughty and Terry Doughty Wildlife Art.

The Winning Attitude: Pg. 42, Betsy Gordon, (photograph), courtesy of the Gordon family.

Evening Bliss in a North Woods: Pg. 44-45, (photograph), fitimi © iStock.com.

Mrs. Sun & Old Man River: Pg. 46-47, (photograph), LarryKnupp © iStock.com.

Sea Gulls: Pg. 48, Tom and Shellie Anthony, (photograph), courtesy of the Anthony family.

God's Amazing Pine Trees: Pg. 49, (photograph), alex5248 © iStock.com.

The Cat's Meow: Pg. 50-51, (photograph), miodrag ignjatovic © iStock.com.

Exercise Today?: Pg. 53, (photograph), JordanSimeonov © iStock.com.

A By-Faith Attitude: Pg. 54, (photograph), StockPhotosArt © iStock.com, Pg. 55, (illustration), cutelittlethings © iStock.com.

Truth: Pg. 56, (photograph), yacobchuk © iStock.com, Pg. 57, (photograph) gzorgz © iStock.com, (photograph) Dmitrich © iStock.com.

Christmas Future: Pg. 58, (photograph), Juanmonino © iStock.com.

A Country Boy's Creed: Pg. 59, (photograph), TomasSerenda © iStock.com.

A North Woods' Storm: Pg. 60-61, (photograph), NaLha © iStock.com.

Loonie Toonies: Pg. 62, (photograph), pchoui © iStock.com.

A Lake's Changing Face: Pg. 65, (photograph), Askar Karimullin © iStock.com.

The Fast Food Lesson: Pg. 66, (photograph), Juanmonino © iStock.com.

Four Great Friends: Pg. 67, (photograph), Ljupco © iStock.com.

Sunset: Pg. 68-69, (photograph), sonatali © iStock.com.

A Quest Fulfilled: Pg. 70-71, (photograph/art), kevron2001 © iStock.com.

Those Big Doctrinal Words: Pg. 72, (photograph), Rastan © iStock.com.

Walking Unaware: Pg. 74, (photograph), TerryJ © iStock.com.

Servant Leadership: Pg. 76, Karl Kroening, (photograph), courtesy of IMMI.

A Prudent Pause: Pg. 78-79, (photograph), Vicu9 © iStock.com.

The Christian's Bar of Soap: Pg. 80, (photograph), Moostocker © iStock.com.

The Old Cable Saying: Pg. 81, (photograph), minddream © iStock.com. Pg. 81, Mann, Horace, "Habit is a Cable" (quote), Graded Selections for Memorizing: Adapted for Use at Home and in School, by John Bradley Peaslee.

House...or Home: Pg. 82-83, (photograph), Milkos © iStock.com.

Bicycle Lore: Pg. 84-85, (photograph), baona © iStock.com.

God's Awesome College Gift: Pg. 86-87, (photograph), Milkos © iStock.com, Pg. 87, (photograph), courtesy of the Anthony family.

Me, Blue and an Old Chair Too: Pg. 88, (photography), Juanmonino © iStock.com.

The Hourglass: Pg. 89, (photograph), Nastco © iStock.com.

Sensing God's Great Love: Pg. 90, (photograph), Choreograph © iStock.com.

Hearing His Voice in Song: Pg. 92, (photograph), pawopa336 © iStock.com, "Jesus Paid it All", (hymn), Elvina M. Hall, 1865, "Blesses Assurance, Jesus is Mine!", (hymn), Frances Crosby, 1873, "How Firm a Foundation, Ye Saints of the Lord", (hymn), George Keith, 1787, "Jesus Loves Me", (hymn), Anna Bartlett Warner, 1860, "The Still Small Voice", (hymn), Thomas O. Chisholm, "Oh How He Loves You and Me"©, (hymn), Kurt Kaiser, 1975 Word Music, LLC.

Captured by a Song: Pg. 93, (photograph), courtesy of the Anthony family.

The Great Park Discovery: Pg. 94-95, (photograph), Bill Sykes © iStock.com, "Jesus Loves Me", (hymn), Anna Bartlett Warner, 1860, poem added to music by William Batchelder Bradbury 1862.

Cynicism: Pg. 96-97, (photograph), BrianAJackson © iStock.com.

Walking with Worry: Pg. 98-99, (photograph), serezniy © iStock.com.

Cloud Play: Pg. 100, (photograph), gollykim © iStock.com.

Self Talk: Pg. 101, (photograph), D-Keine © iStock.com.

The Magic Old Bench: Pg. 102-103, (photograph), LUMIKK555 © iStock.com, Pg. 102, James Richard Anthony, (photographs) courtesy of the Anthony family, Pg. 103, (illustration), cutelittlethings © iStock.com.

The Long View: Pg. 104, (photograph), MGSmith © iStock.com.

What's in a Name: Pg. 106, (photograph), Rawpixel © iStock.com, (photograph) artisteer © iStock.com.

Arrogance Uncovered: Pg. 107, (photograph), -Antonio- © iStock.com.

Dream Flights: Pg. 108-109, (photograph), sdominick © iStock.com.

None to Son: Pg. 110-111, (photograph), zhaojiankang © iStock.com, (photograph), BrianAJackson © iStock.com.

Soul Searching: Pg. 112-113, (photograph), ipopba © iStock.com.

The Chime's Magic Helpers: Pg. 114, Byron Jackson (art), courtesy of Byron Jackson artist.

Captured by the Sea: Pg. 115, (photograph), mihtiander © iStock.com.

Birth of a Business: Pg. 117, (photograph), Weedezign © iStock.com.

The Old Fisherman's Rhyme: Pg. 118-119, (photograph) EduardHarkonen © iStock.com. Mary Beth Moster, (family photograph), courtesy of Anthony family, Pg. 119, (illustration), ulimi © iStock.com, paraphrased fishing proverb of unknown origin, referenced by Forest E. Condor, Fisherman's Bible, 1952. Frank C. Brown Collection of North Carolina Folklore, 1964.

To See by the Sea: Pg. 120, (photograph), slavadubrovin © iStock.com.

Sands of Time: Pg. 121, (photograph), f9photos © iStock.com.

Snow Dreaming: Pg. 123, (photograph), EvgeniiAnd © iStock.com, (photography) Samohin © iStock.com.

The Rocking Chair's Passion: Pg. 124, (photograph), courtesy of the Anthony family, Pg. 125, (photograph), courtesy of the Anthony family.

Bicycling Through Time: Pg. 126-127, (photograph), Grafner © iStock.com.

A Message from my Ancestors: Pg. 129, (photograph), NoDerog © iStock.com.

North Woods' Pancakes: Pg. 130, (photograph), lauraag © iStock.com.

The Wee Little Chair's Hope: Pg. 131, (photograph), courtesy of the Anthony family.

Ode to Odin: Pg. 132-133, (photograph), Quirky Mundo © iStock.com, Shellie Anthony, (photograph), courtesy of the Anthony family, Pg. 132, (illustration), cutelittlethings © iStock.com.

The Awesome Campus Walk: Pg. 134-135, (photograph), Blueline, IU Bloomington Campus, Sample Gates, courtesy of IU Alumni Association, October 30, 2018.

Unbroken Family Circle: Pg. 136-137, (illustration), VasjaKoman © iStock.com.

The Stone's Witness: Pg. 139, (photograph), THEPALMER © iStock.com.

Blessed Assurance Passed On: Pg. 140-141, (photograph), RishVintage © iStock.com.

Ann's Song: Pg. 143, (photograph), Halfpoint © iStock.com, Pg. 143, (illustration), cutelittlethings © iStock.com.

A Sailor's Dream Fulfilled: Pg. 144, (photograph), dmbaker © iStock.com.

Smile Power: Pg. 146, (photograph), vadimguzhva © iStock.com.